Introductions in
Feminist Theology

9

WITHDRAWN

Editorial Committee

Mary Grey
Lisa Isherwood
Janet Wootton

Sheffield Academic Press
A Continuum imprint

Introducing Feminist Cultural Hermeneutics

An African Perspective

Musimbi R.A. Kanyoro

Copyright © 2002 Sheffield Academic Press
A Continuum imprint

Published by Sheffield Academic Press Ltd
The Tower Building, 11 York Road, London SE1 7NX
370 Lexington Avenue, New York NY 10017–6550

www.SheffieldAcademicPress.com
www.continuumbooks.com

British Library Cataloguing-in-Publication Data
A catalogue record for this book is available from the British Library

Typeset by Sheffield Academic Press
Printed on acid-free paper in Great Britain by MPG Books Ltd, Bodmin, Cornwall

ISBN 0-8264-6054-2

Table of Contents

Preface   vii

Chapter One

Introduction: The Beginnings of a Story   1
     Vulnerability and Community   1
     First Story: Child Marriage   5
     Second Story: Fidelity   7
     Overview of the Project   9

Chapter Two

The Problem: What Is the Story?   13
     Synopsis of the African Woman's Dilemma   13
     First Story: Infibulation   15
     Second Story: Barrenness   15
     Gender as a Concept of Cultural Analysis   17
     Cultural Hermeneutics as a Key to Reading the Bible in Africa   18
     Background of the Community Studied   20

Chapter Three

Methodology: The Telling of the Story   23
     Contextual Challenges   23
     African Women Doing Communal Theology   27
     A Safe Place to Speak for Ourselves   29

Chapter Four

Research Project: The Story   32
     The Book of Ruth in Women's Theologies   32
     The Festival on Ruth   38
     Reading the Bible as 'Own Text'   41
     Reflection on Experience   49

Chapter Five
Cultural Hermeneutics: The Meaning of the Story   58
    Cultural Hermeneutics: A Key to African Women's Liberation   58
    Cultural Hermeneutics: A Method of Sifting the Usable Culture   66

Chapter Six
Engendered Cultural Hermeneutics: The Power of the Story   79
    Accountability: An Issue for the Church in Africa   79
    Accountability: An Issue for Women in Africa   83
    Accountability: An Issue for Churchwomen's Organizations   87
    Accountability: An Issue for African Women Theologians   88

Bibliography   95
Index of References   100
Index of Authors   101

Preface

I dedicate this book to my mother in memory of my father

This book was first written as a dissertation for the Feminist Doctor of Ministry Programme at San Francisco Theological Seminary of San Anselmo, in California. The dissertation was presented in 1998 and recognised for an outstanding award. Thanks are due to the San Francisco Theological Seminary, and specifically to Professor Walt Davis for his commitment to the Feminist Ministry Programme, to my project supervisor, Professor Letty Russell, and project reader, Mercy Amba Oduyoye. My appreciation also goes to Shannon Clarkson, Jacqueline Urfer and Ana Villanueva for their help in copy editing. I have made various presentations in different forums on aspects of my research. I am grateful to all those who have encouraged me to publish this work in the form of a book.

I am delighted to bring the voices of rural women in Bware into the public debate of theology and to them I say 'Thank-you' for motivating me and allowing me to discuss issues that are paramount to the liberation of women in general and to women in Africa in particular. The impact of this research continually provides me with the motivation to do ever more feminist analysis of gender-based justice.

My greatest appreciation goes to my husband, daughter and son who constantly give me space to continue writing and researching and travelling to share with others issues that make us all truly human. In 1980 when I graduated with a PhD in Linguistics, none of the three members of my family were there, but in 1998 when I graduated with a Doctor of Ministry at the San Francisco Theological Seminary they were all present. They celebrated with me and together we accepted the recognition of honor awarded to this research by the Seminary.

Finally, but not least, I owe a huge debt of thanks to my mother for having given birth and raised seven girls and three boys. I consider my mother to be an emblem of the women whose lives are the subject of this book.

Musimbi Kanyoro
May 2002

Chapter One

Introduction: The Beginnings of a Story

The expression 'doing theology' is a conscious statement which describes the method of action–reflection out of which theological reflections arise, rather than simply applying existing theological insights to present situations. This method invites communal theology. It is in a group where the action and reflection take place and where the religious experience finds its communal experience. The community of Bware has been for me the location for doing theology. The experience of sitting with women in my community and hearing one another began a new phase in my life. It was in this village of Bware in 1994 that I began to ask questions which led to the research project of this study. It all began in the context of women's vulnerability.

Vulnerability and Community

My village, Bware, is tucked safely and securely away from the hustles of fast life, in the countryside of Western Kenya. No deadlines, no fixed agendas and a lot of company. In July of 1994, I went back to my home village to mourn the death of my father. After the burial of my father, I decided to spend the rest of the summer vacation with my mother and the whole village. The school, the small dispensary and the Church which I helped build are the landmarks of my village. This rural community where my parents retired to has no shopping mall, no library, no post office or telephone and no public transportation. In this serenity, having mourned and buried my loving father, my thoughts flew back and forth to Nairobi, to Geneva and to the world. I reminisced about the people, books and activities that made my days in those places. I was often overcome with turbulent unrest, longing for something different and far away that my village did not offer me. Some mornings, I woke up longing for a newspaper, but everybody in my village lives without print and visual media. In Bware, the radio is a treasure of great value.

The community of Bware constantly struggles to be connected to the rest of Kenya. We all walk five kilometers to the nearest public road where we may get transportation to a hospital, a post office, a bank, a shopping center, and of course catch the bus to the big city of Nairobi. The journey from Bware to Nairobi takes eight hours by bus, which is exactly the same amount of time it takes to travel from Geneva to Nairobi by air. The public buses are few and usually so crowded with passengers that the use of the expression 'sardines in a can' is not even a befitting image. The buses move so fast that their speed separates body and soul, and it takes some doing to rejoin the two should one make it to their destination. Many bodies have arrived without souls, and an equal number of souls misplace their bodies. That is, my village and our efforts to be connected to the rest of the world are often punctuated by daily loss of life through road accidents. In addition many children die from malaria and other curable diseases, women die in childbirth, and deaths of various types occur due to sheer distance from medical centers exacerbated by lack of public transportation.

In the summer of 1994, in the context of sadness and vulnerability, I acknowledged that my values have changed. Living away from Bware I had developed different concerns and priorities, ways of analysis, and general lifestyle. I needed courage and sincerity to accept that although I was born in Bware, my social location[1] was no longer Bware. My material and economic status was different, my worldview asked for things different from those offered by my village, my explanation of daily issues was completely out of line with the reality of Bware. I began for the first time to accept that I had changed by staying away from Bware and I needed to acknowledge that in order to free myself to be curious, to ask questions, and to listen to the answers without assuming that I knew the drumbeat of Bware, my birth home.

I left for boarding school at the age of twelve and continued to study away from home, both in secondary school and later at the University of Nairobi, returning home more or less as a visitor during vacations. In 1976, after completing my undergraduate studies, I proceeded to graduate school in the USA and had no physical presence in Bware until 1982 when I returned to my home country, Kenya. But then I settled permanently in Nairobi, set-up a home of my own and started a continental job that took me to much of Africa and the rest of the world and far away from Bware. I no longer consistently went for vacations in Bware, but rather for very brief occasional visits to the

---

1.   See Mary Ann Tolbert, 'The Politics and Poetics of Location', in Fernando Segovia and Mary Ann Tolbert (eds.), *Reading from this Place: Social Location and Biblical Interpretation in the United States* (Minneapolis: Fortress Press, 1995), pp. 305-17.

family. In 1988, I moved to Geneva, Switzerland, and took up an international and global job with such an intensive travelling schedule that the occasional visits to Bware became reduced even further. Thus, for 18 years I had lived in different environments and settings on three continents and travelled the world over. These have been the key formative years during which I have done my studies, developed a social and political nuance, affirmed my womanhood, encountered theological formation, and become self-reliant in socio-economic matters. All of the above named factors shaped my worldview and they prompted me to ask whether Bware was home for me and if not, where then is home for me? The discomfort of the realization that I would always be a foreigner in my village as I am one in Geneva is a shock that many of us, popularly called 'ecumenical or international migrants', resist accepting.

In their book, *Biblical Interpretation: A Road Map*, Frederick C. Tiffany and Sharon H. Ringe advise Bible interpreters to 'begin at home', meaning where you are located.[2] Such an approach requires the interpreter to be sure of what 'home' means to her. Bware is my birth home, but is it also my theological home? The things I share with the community in Bware are far more than what I share with people with whom I have studied theology. In Bware I feel at home because we speak the same language, eat the same food, walk the same roads, laugh at each other's jokes and know how to be vulnerable together. It is for these reasons that I claim Bware not only as my birth home but also my theological home, for theology is but a tool to help me tell the story of God's doing in Bware.

In 1994, I wanted my homecoming to be lived in a full and enriching way. I knew I had changed from the days when I was there as a small girl, and I did not assume that life had always been static in my village for those who stayed. My yearning was to create space for mutual sharing. I wanted to share with the community in my village the treasure that I had discovered while away from them. I wanted to learn from them about what it means to live and experience Christ in this place, which would be described as 'isolated'. Thus, I began to redirect my mother's friends, who had come to comfort her, into a theologizing group of women. They came every day in the afternoon after work on the farm as our culture prompted them to do for a bereaved widow. These meetings, which had no streamlined agenda, took on a new image as we began to intentionally schedule in a new purpose. We gathered to just talk with one another and to read the Scriptures together. We talked about our families, our farms, cattle, ceremonies, weddings and funerals, churches; this list is not

2.   See Frederick C. Tiffany and Sharon H. Ringe, *Biblical Interpretation: A Road Map* (Nashville: Abingdon Press, 1996).

exhaustive. The non-systemization and order of priority is reflected in the way this list is presented. So we talked, we read Scriptures, we sang and became friends through sharing. It was good in the beginning, but it became hard and painful as we dared to trust one another and open our hearts to each other in the safety of mutual vulnerability. The painful process began by the growing awareness of our own situation as women and as women of Bware.

As we talked under a tree in the front yard of my birth home, my mother's new and fresh status as a widow made her vulnerability rather obvious. Such vulnerability silently solicited solidarity and mutuality. Each of the women felt the need to offer some words of comfort to my mother and the only way to enter into such conversation was for the participants to expose their own vulnerability. Therefore, each one of the women who came to comfort my vulnerable mother felt safe to let her own vulnerability also be known. The conversations moved from one subject to another, encompassing both the private and public, and soon they found a home base in talking about family, relationships and the role of the Church.

Amazing stories of pain and sorrow, joy and jubilation were part of the menu with no barriers built and nothing but that kind of mutual vulnerability. Quaker, Roman Catholic, Pentecostal and Seventh Day Adventist are the dominant churches in my village. Women present came from all of these churches and there were also those who were not church members because of their 'family situation'. This is a euphemism which in church language means that the women may be in a polygamous marriage, single mothers, single women, widows and all other women whose life is seen not to be good enough for church membership. Casually, without anyone eliciting the information, in the safety of a home with ears to listen that were not those of church leaders, the women spoke about their lives, telling life stories that revealed their marginalization by our socio-cultural systems and by the Church. One after the other, we spoke about illnesses in our lives and in our families. We spoke about the children and their various needs. For some, it was the struggle to get school fees, while for others, it was the reality of choices. Women have to make a choice for the girl child to stay at home because the family cannot maintain all of the children in school. They have to choose not to seek medical help for themselves so that the available resources can be used for the healthcare of their children. They have to make a choice not to confront their husbands over all issues in order to save the marriage from breaking up. They uncovered so many hidden emotions of pain and hurt. Yet, rather than seeing these things as endless struggles, the women of Bware sing and depend on the God of the Bible, as well as all other beliefs, for hope. Their hope is as solid as a rock. That is what sustains them.

The naming of the pain of women in my village is done with realism and without self-pity. The women of Bware believe in themselves and they illustrate that vulnerability is not weakness. The fact that everyone was able to share her story while others listened was also the key to mutual risk that women of Bware take as they continue to affirm life through their choices and their actions. In my home village I learned that culture must not be romanticized. It was necessary for us to come to terms with identifying in our cultures those things that were beautiful and wholesome and life-affirming and to denounce those which were denying us life and wholeness. In ecumenical language, the above event was about the coming together of women of faith whom Christ had come to free from the bondage of illness, poverty, patriarchy and cultural practices that dehumanize women. As we shared our stories, sisters, mothers, grandmothers, co-wives, women of all ages and sizes, I lamented that the theological reflections of women in the ecumenical setting are poorer without these voices of rural African women. I yearned to bring their voices to the ecumenical theological tables of the world. I would never have imagined some of the stories I heard from these 'my mothers, aunts, sisters and grandmothers' that I had known for so long.

Here are just a couple of examples.

First Story: Child Marriage

Makungu is a woman in her early forties and a mother of five boys and three girls. She talked about her daughter Mebo. Mebo had been attending the local school until just a few months ago when she became pregnant. Mebo named her teacher as the man who had made her pregnant. Mebo was sent out of school. At the time of the conversation, Makungu had a heavy heart. An older man, a widower, had come to the family with an offer to marry Mebo.

Makungu did not want Mebo to marry this older person, but she felt trapped in a situation where she was not the only decision-maker. The whole clan saw this as the only opportunity for Mebo to get a husband because, 'it is our culture that every girl must get married'. If she does not get married, she will become a laughing stock of the family. The family name, which is now soiled with her pregnancy outside marriage, will be ruined further if Mebo 'ages inside the house'. The local expression translates as 'if Mebo becomes of age without moving to a husband, then she will need a place to stay and inheritance cannot be shared with her brothers'. Besides, it is expected that women should be buried in their husbands' homes, not their birth homes. So the dilemma for Makungu was that if she rejected the offer, her family would not support her and she alone would not be able to support Mebo without the support of the household.

As the group discussed, they too seemed to be caught in the cultural trap and it is at this point that I clearly saw difference between my view on the issue and that of all the other women of Bware. Although all the women were aware of the dilemma that Makungu faced, the group did not seem to want to come up with alternative suggestions that were out of the norm. When I suggested that Mebo could remain single, have her baby and return to school, they told me that the schools would not admit her. I tried to suggest that we should take the teacher responsible for Mebo's pregnancy to court for child-abuse, rape and ruining Mebo's life forever. The group not only rejected this option but they responded that nothing would happen to the teacher, much less would the action take away the shame of Mebo's pregnancy. I suggested that we organize to challenge the system which does not hold men who ruin the lives of young women accountable. There was no support for this idea and in fact it seemed as if I suddenly was speaking a foreign language. In this pathetic apathy, everyone seemed preoccupied with finding reasons to justify Mebo's marriage.

The conversation then took a different direction. It shifted from providing cultural answers to providing biblical and church answers to the cultural question. One of the women pointed to the fact that the biblical Ruth had married an older man. Therefore, she reasoned, it was not such a strange or bad idea for Mebo to marry this older man either. One of them took the Bible and read aloud these words of Boaz to Ruth: 'May you be blessed by the Lord my daughter… You have not gone after young men poor or rich, And now my daughter, don't be afraid, I will do for you all that you ask…'[3]

Having read this piece of Scripture, the women seemed comforted to go on and encourage Makungu to let her daughter get married to an older man.

This incident left me disturbed and amazed. In my home village the women were reading exactly the same texts that other ecumenical women and feminist theologians read. However, reading from within a different cultural and social context made a lot of difference to the hermeneutics of those texts. For the last 18 years, I had been mostly hearing women challenge interpretations of the Bible that diminish women. Here, I was hearing women affirm and justify a reading of the text of Ruth that has potential harm to women and girls. It was reasoned that because such a reading enhanced our culture, then it was good for us. It is a fact that African cultures have more similarities with the cultures of ancient biblical times, than with contemporary Western, secularized cultures, even though communities in Africa have daily contact with Western

3.   Ruth 3.10-11. All biblical quotations are from the NRSV (Division of Christian Education of the National Council of the Churches of Christ in the USA, 1989).

cultures through media, books, schools, churches and the government. But to use the text of the Bible to validate any culture is a highly suspicious action. What if both the biblical cultures and the culture in question have inherent injustices in them? Injustice is never right, not even if it is in the Bible. Such a statement, though, moves the debate to questions of the authority of the Bible. The women of Bware in 1994 were not ready to debate the authority of the Bible, let alone the authority of culture. It was my turn to learn from their own methods. Rather than feeling anger or self-pity for the way my ideas were rejected, I had to make the choice not to pursue my solutions but rather to develop a relationship which enables us to continue discussing these issues of life and death in our village.

Second Story: Fidelity

> Ajagira's husband was known in the village for his infidelity. In the group, Ajagira shared her pain about this issue, showing her fears that she might get AIDS through her husband. The other women listened and then each talked about their fear of AIDS. Within a short time, however, they all resorted to excusing the men by use of culture. 'Men will always be men. They can do what they wish. If a woman becomes foolish and copies them, families will break. This is our culture; it is only God who can protect us from AIDS.' A devout woman, the leader of the women's organization in one of the churches, started to quote Scripture that talked about God protecting people from dangerous incidents. She quoted God's protection of the Israelites in the desert where even poisonous snakes did not bite them (Deut. 8.15-16). She said that those who fear and honor God will be protected from any danger, even that of AIDS.

The community of African Christian rural women of Bware village described above hold the Bible in awe as the word of God written directly to them. When they read the Bible, they read and hear the message as if it were written specifically for them. They do not dwell on the text as somebody else's text to be read and analyzed, but rather they see the purpose of the text as providing them with a framework to look at their own lives. They immediately appropriate the text and situate themselves inside of it, trying to understand what is expected of them in that particular text. Given, for example, the texts of Jesus' healing miracles, the women see themselves as 'those who came to Jesus bringing their sick or their own sickness' (Lk. 7.1-10; Mt. 15.21-28; Mk. 7.31-38). Thus, discussing a text really means discussing the life of the people without making any great distinction between method and content. Reality and the biblical text merge and become one, each shedding light on the other and competing for attention. This is where culture comes into play and it will be illustrated by the community Bible study on the book of Ruth (pp. 32-57 below).

The rural women of Bware read the Bible for assurance and for answers to their questions and dilemmas. They read the same Scripture passages used by feminist theologians and other Christian women. The women of Bware love to read the story of Ruth and the stories of other women in the Bible. Some of the stories in the Bible embarrassed them. When we read the story popularly known as 'The Story of the Woman Caught in Adultery' (Jn 8.3-11) many said they thought that this story elicits shame and depicts women as the unfaithful ones. Although they admitted to silently questioning why the man who was with her was not equally condemned, they did not dare ask their question loudly in a church-convened Bible study.

This reading of the Bible and living a life of struggle with a determined hope is a way of doing a theology of life. But how do we discern the Spirit of God at work in cultures? The reality of the women of Bware was strongly founded on the interaction between Scripture and life experiences, which are cultural. The task of acknowledging the positive values of cultures and their role in God's working in theology defined itself as the immediate need for the communal theology we were doing together as women of Bware. Women of Bware are willing to imagine and speculate on the things both said and unsaid in the Scriptures.[4] Thus in so doing, the women of rural Africa are themselves a resource in the search for their liberation. But how may this energy and possibility for self-liberation be nurtured to fruition among the women of Bware? How may it be used to affirm that far from being the helpless victims of hunger, poverty, exploitation and disease as they are often portrayed, women of rural Africa are God's daughters in search of abundant life? I felt that something different needed to be done in the way the Bible is read by women in my village. My mind could not be constrained to just accepting the use of the Bible to justify that which causes dilemmas to the women of Bware. Hearing these stories and leaving them where they had concluded seemed incomplete. I was yearning to engage them in more talk, to ask them to be angry and to make some new decisions, but I could not find the method

---

4.   In 1993, American women held a mid-decade conference on the theme 'Women Re-Imagining God'. The ecumenical setting and presence of women allowed for several imaginations that could change the Church. But alas! The conference was condemned by right-wing Christians, and the women were seen as feminists and not Christians, for it is believed by some that you cannot be both. This false belief assumes that what women do under feminist theology is not theology but trash.

to do it. I was convinced that the Church must reflect on culture, but I did not know how to effect it.

As I pondered how to awaken something new in Bware, it dawned on me that everything in my village is explained through the eyes of culture. Even the Bible is read through the lens of culture. Our cultural heritage was indeed the basis for our common understanding about who we are and what that means. It seemed to imply that for our community in Bware, if change were to be viable for anything, it must address first and foremost, cultural issues. This premonition led me to suggest that our culture needs to be put to a thorough test under the framework of what I later came to call 'cultural hermeneutics'.

'Hermeneutics' literally means 'interpretation'. Biblical hermeneutics, as a theological subject, permits people from one generation to another to re-interpret scriptural texts in the light of their times and culture. All inter-pretations bear the bias of the interpreters. The context of a person affects the meaning attached to any communication event, verbal or otherwise.[5] The semantic value of symbols and words is culturally determined. Every reading of a text represents the reality of a particular people situated in a particular time and space. Because culture is so central to people's thought systems, it needs to be analyzed too. Cultural hermeneutics therefore refers to the analy-sis and interpretation of how culture conditions people's understanding of reality at a particular time and location.

Overview of the Project

The entry point of the study of this project is the reading of the book of Ruth with women from my home village. The purpose of the study is to investigate our culture, but rather than beginning with the culture and making partici-pants feel accused, the study uses the book of Ruth as a step towards identifying cultural issues that need to be discussed by the Bware group. This study singles out culture as an important key to reading the Bible in Africa and its analysis as vital to the lives of African women. Such a thesis is not altogether new; as many African theologians have stated before, the belief system and culture are integrated.[6] The new feature that this study contributes

---

5.   See Severino J. Croato's 'Introduction', in his *Biblical Hermeneutics: Toward a Theory of Reading as the Production of Meaning* (trans. Robert R. Bart; Maryknoll, NY: Orbis Books, 1995), p. 1.

6.   See, for example, Benezet Bujo, *African Theology in its Social Context* (Maryknoll, NY: Orbis Books, 1994); Rosino Gibellini, *Paths of African Theology* (Maryknoll, NY: Orbis Books, 1994); Simon Maimela, *Culture, Religion and Liberation* (Pretoria: Penrose Books, 1994);

to African theology is the clear call for an analysis of culture as a means of seeking justice and liberation for women in Africa. It advocates cultural hermeneutics as a paradigm of a gender-sensitive African theology.

To use the Bible as a beginning point is a legitimate step for the women of Bware. The awe that rural women in Africa have for the Bible and for religion means that they take the Bible seriously. For example, they will argue that levirate marriages are good because they are in the Bible. To differ in matters of culture is a 'taboo', a word that in people's minds translates as bringing death to the family and to the community. This is where the tasks lie for those of us reading the Bible from those cultures that closely mirror the times and practices similar to those in the Bible. We can quickly rush to justify our behavior simply because we think we are in good company with the biblical culture. On the other hand, those cultures that are far removed from biblical culture risk reading the Bible as fiction. Cultural hermeneutics puts *every culture* to scrutiny with the intention of testing its liberative potential for people at different times in history.

I argue that the culture of the reader in Africa has more influence on the way the biblical text is understood and used in communities than the historical facts about the text. This leads me to suggest that not knowing the nuances of the culture of modern readers of the Bible has more far-reaching reper-cussions to biblical hermeneutics than is normally acknowledged. I further hypothesize that cultural hermeneutics is a prerequisite to biblical hermen-eutics and therefore a necessary tool for those who teach homiletics and pastoral work in the seminaries, and an indispensable tool for Bible translators, preachers and teachers of ministry and theology (see Chapter 2). I have come to this conclusion through the experience of working with Bible translators in Africa and also occasional reading of the Bible with other rural African women in Kenya, Tanzania, Eastern Zaire, Rwanda and Burundi between 1982 and 1996 during my employment with United Bible Socities. African Christians are ardent Bible believers. Whenever a Christian family owns one or two books, those books are likely to be a hymnal and a Bible.[7] They read or listen

Emmanuel Martey, *African Theology: Inculturation and Liberation* (Maryknoll, NY: Orbis Books, 1993); J.N.K. Mugambi and Laurenti Magesa (eds.), *The Church in African Christianity* (AACC African Challenges Series; Nairobi: Initiatives, 1990); John Parrat, *Reinventing Christianity: African Theology Today* (Grand Rapids: Eerdmans, 1995); John S. Pobee, *Towards an African Theology* (Nashville: Abingdon Press, 1979); Ernest R. Wendland, *The Culture Factor in Bible Translation: A Study of Communicating the Word of God in a Central African Context* (London: United Bible Societies, 1987).

7.   I carried out a research project with families in western Kenya in 1978 and that was

to the Bible through church-organized occasions as well as by reading it themselves, if and when they are literate.

Secondly, this is a study about theological methodology. It is not a study about the book of Ruth, but rather, the book of Ruth is used as the project from which learning has been drawn. The reading of the book of Ruth has clearly indicated how the experiences of African rural women illuminate biblical interpretation, and at the same time, how issues of culture found in the book of Ruth pose questions to communities in Africa and in particular to the Church (see Chapters 2 and 3).

This is also a study about the significance of oral media as a source of learning for theologians. Although originally the most legitimate form of communication, oral media were overtaken by print media when people began to immortalize the written word as the source of truth. The power of the written word then created the marginalization of a majority of the world's populations who were not literate in the alphabet and in the major languages of power and colonization. The result is the exclusion of the contributions of non-literate communities from the recorded story of faith formation. This study is a reminder to the Church that the original sources of the biblical texts were oral. On matters of faith, justice requires that the experiences of rural communities and of women be included in the interpretation of meaning of the texts of the Bible. In her book *Household of Freedom*, Letty Russell argues that no theology is adequate if it cannot speak to and from the experiences of its participants, its doers and its hearers. Women's experiences include the biological and cultural experiences of being female as well as the feminist experience, the political experience of those who advocate a change of society to include both women and men as human beings.[8] Through this work, we the women of rural Africa are asking something new from the theological debate in general and from women's theology in particular (Chapter 4). A majority of African women have not yet learned to read and write, but they are not lacking in experience. The purpose of this work is to bring the voices of rural African women to bear on the theological thinking of scholars, both women and men. In 1984, the World Council of Churches (WCC) held a consultation in Riano, Italy, on 'Gospel and Culture'. A plea was made for scholars of theology and ecumenics and leaders of churches to design ways to show, 'how people at local levels can enter into the discussion on Gospel and Culture'. It called for methods on

what I found. See Rachel Angogo Kanyoro, *Unity in Diversity: A Linguistic Survey of the ABALUHYIA of Western Kenya* (Vienna: Beiträge zur Afrikanistik, 20, 1983).

8.   Letty M. Russell, *Household of Freedom* (Philadelphia: Westminster Press, 1987).

'how to assist persons in local congregations, villages, rural areas, etc., to participate in this discussion which has much impact on their lives'.[9]

In some ways, this study responds to that plea. It calls for theological under-standing and accommodation of diversity (Chapter 4). Culture is the leading issue that has preoccupied African theology. I write as an African woman and I include myself in identifying with many of the cultural issues that I describe in this study. Thus, I write from within and that is reflected in the way I use inclusive pronouns, such as 'we' and 'us', which violates the rules of academia. I am part of this story and must write from within.

9.   S. Wesley Ariarajah, *Gospel and Culture: An Ongoing Discussion in the Ecumenical Move-ment* (Geneva: WCC Publications, 1994), p. 42.

Chapter Two

The Problem: What Is the Story?

Synopsis of the African Woman's Dilemma

My continent Africa is a land of proverbial wealth; that is, Africa is a land wealthy in proverbs. One of my favorite ones relates the dilemma of the hyena. The hyena was following the general direction of the aroma of barbecuing meat. He wanted a share of this enticing and mouth-watering meat. Suddenly his path forked into two. He was not sure which one would lead him to the meat. In his uncertainty, he put his legs astride the two paths and tried to walk along both and oops! The poor hyena split in the middle. Alas!

The African Christian often walks with one foot in African religion and culture and another in the church and western culture. While the former is condemned as evil and traditional, the latter is passed for good and gospel. The dilemma of the African Christian cannot simply be wished away, especially today when it seems as if the center does not hold and things are falling apart.[1] Christian women of Africa are a part of these two worlds. Often times, one feels the strain of splitting apart when trying to correlate the pull of the culture on the one hand and that of the church on the other. The tension between the notion that it is possible and desirable to live by the gospel without culture is a belief held with much wishful thinking. However, reality tells a different story.

Culture is a double-edged sword. In some instances, culture is like the creed for the community identity. In other instances, culture is the main justification for difference, oppression and injustice—especially to those whom culture defines as 'the other', 'the outsider'. Both feminist theology and African theology are only beginning to come to grips with culture and religion, while traditionalists have already tainted our understanding of culture by defending cultural practices harmful to women. New voices from the perspec-

---

1.   See Chinua Achebe, *Things Fall Apart* (London: Heinemann, 1964).

tive of African women are providing a detailed analysis of the issues of culture and religion in Africa, among them are authors Oduyoye,[2] Oduyoye and Kanyoro,[3] Maimela,[4] Pobee[5] and Gibellini.[6] What these scholars find is that cultural issues preoccupy African liberation theology in a similar manner as race relations do African-American liberation theology.

There are profound difficulties in seeking the liberation of culture in Africa. African culture is perceived to be the thread which strings the community beliefs and social set-up together. It is therefore a great threat to community security to be critical of culture, for there are elements in these cultures which are the very veins through which the solidarity of communities is nurtured. In the African indigenous thought system, culture and religion are not distinct from each other. In fact, the conversations which took place in my mother's garden under a mango tree (referred to above), gave meaning to the cliché that in Africa there is no distinction between the sacred and the secular, the spiritual and the material, the natural and the supernatural. One seeks in vain for terms and concepts in African languages which refer to these distinctions or convey these conceptions. Such terms as exist now in this regard are borrowed.[7]

Therefore, culture and religion in Africa are one and the same thing: they embrace all areas of one's total life. There is no sphere of existence that is excluded from the double grip of culture and religion. The presence or absence of rain, the well-being of the community, sexuality, marriage, birthing, naming children, success or failure, the place and form of one's burial, among others, all come under the scope of religion and culture.

Having stated this, it must also be said that African ways of living and being are not static, just as no culture or religion can ever claim to be static. Hence, culture and religion in Africa today, while bearing a direct link to the past, have adapted themselves out of necessity to present realities. They have had to contend with contact from other cultures through colonial occupation, contact with Christianity, and contact with Western culture and its technological artifacts. In addition, African religions and cultures have had to

See Mercy Amba Oduyoye, *Daughters of Anowa: African Women and Patriarchy* (Maryknoll, NY: Orbis Books, 1995).

3.   See Mercy Amba Oduyoye and Musimbi R.A. Kanyoro (eds.), *The Will to Arise: Women, Tradition and Church in Africa* (Maryknoll, NY: Orbis Books, 1992).

4.   See Simon Maimela, *Culture, Religion and Liberation* (Pretoria: Penrose Books, 1994).

5.   See John S. Pobee, *Towards an African Theology* (Nashville: Abingdon Press, 1979).

6.   See Rosino Gibellini, *Paths of African Theology* (Maryknoll, NY: Orbis Books, 1994).

7.   E.E. Evans-Pritchard, *Theories of Primitive Religion* (London: Oxford University Press, 1965), p. 65.

contend with new political realities, the formation of new identities, and interaction with the surrounding and new-contact cultures and religions. Despite such encounters, it amazes both Africans and foreigners alike to see how alive and well cultural practices in Africa are alive and well despite their hospitality to new encounters.

Women in Africa are the custodians of cultural practices. For generations, women have guarded cultural prescriptions strictly governed by the fear of breaking taboos. Many aspects which diminish women continue to be practiced to various degrees, often making women objects of cultural preservation. Harmful traditional practices are passed on as 'cultural values' and therefore are not to be discussed, challenged or changed. In the guise of culture, harmful practices and traditions are perpetuated. Practices such as female genital mutilation, early betrothals and marriages, and the stigmatization of single women, barren women and widows are not liberating to women. Yet it is in fact women who sustain these practices. Issues of this nature illustrate the reality of women's vulnerability in the face of cultural prescriptions.

In both the private and public spheres, the roles and images of African women are socially and culturally defined. Within this framework of operation, women have been socialized into a state of numbness where questioning the cultural is perceived to be a dangerous trend. Culture silences many women in Africa and makes it impossible for them to experience the liberating promises of God of which the Bible speaks. The stories of women in African culture are cause for concern. Listen to some of them as told by women of courage and vulnerability.

First Story: Infibulation

I came back to the hospital a week after delivery because I could not hold urine. The doctors have not yet helped me even though I have had two operations. They say that it is because of the infibulation I had when I was ten years. I am now sixteen years and this was my first birth. There was no money for school fees, so I did not go beyond primary class six. My parents arranged for this marriage. My husband is more than forty years and he has two other wives. I am the youngest.[8]

Second Story: Barrenness

I was married at the age of 19 immediately after completing secondary school. We had a beautiful church wedding and I continued teaching Sunday school in

---

8.   Amina, interviewed by author, in a hospital in Mombasa, Kenya, 27 December 1992.

my new church just as I had done in the church where I grew up. When I could not conceive within six months, the women began to ask me what was wrong. After one year, still there was no sign of pregnancy. My sisters-in-law started to make up stories that I had been a loose woman and had abortions before marriage. That was very upsetting to me because I had never had any sex with anyone before marriage. My husband was the only man I knew.

During the second year, my husband started coming home late and finding fault with me for everything. If he knocked the door and I did not run to open it, he would call me lazy and punch me. His whole family also insulted me in many ways. I talked to the pastor, but he simply told me to persevere and not do anything to annoy my husband. He also told me to repent my past sins and remember the man is the head of the home. I went to many different doctors who said that they could not identify what was wrong with me. The doctors asked that both my husband and I should seek medical help. For a long time, I could not dare suggest to my husband about going to the doctor. One day I did and my fears were justified. He beat me thoroughly for suspecting him.

Life became unbearable and I decided to return to my parents' home. My mother was always embarrassed by my situation, so she did not like to talk about it. She welcomed me all right, but never said anything to comfort me from the situation I was running away from. My father never talked to me about it, but he may have discussed with mother. He never looked at me. Whenever he wanted me to do something, he would tell my mother to tell me. There were lots of chores in the house for the evenings and early mornings.

I worked on my father's farm daily but my brothers and their wives frequently insulted me. They said that my hard work was aimed at winning my father's favor so that he could give me a piece of land as inheritance. They warned that I had no rights to family land as a woman and I should find a husband so that I would inherit through his lineage. Each of my brothers swore that they would not even bury my body on their pieces of land. If I answered back in protest, everybody including mother would tell me not to be rude to my brothers when they are the owners of the home where I was simply getting free lodging. I protested to my mother about these insults. She listened silently and simply said that she would talk to my brothers. In reality, she never did. After some time, I debated whether to kill myself or just leave home to nowhere. I decided on the latter.

I have done many odd jobs to earn a living here in Mombasa. The only time I had a sexual friendship, I became pregnant, so I have one child, but I do not like to live a life of looseness. I repented and went back to the church. However, the Church cannot accept me as a full member because I am not married and I had a child out of wedlock. I love my daughter. I live for her. I want her to get an education because I want her to have a better future. I am happy with my work as a cleaner in this hotel. We cleaners have to be very honest because we lose our jobs if a guest's property is stolen or messed up. I have been doing this job for 18 years.[9]

9.   Aliviza, interviewed by author, at a tourist beach hotel, Mombasa, Kenya, 27 December 1992.

Gender as a Concept of Cultural Analysis

If today African women are able to name the oppressive aspects of African cultures, it has not come easily. Telling these stories of dehumanizing cultural practices is still rare and a struggle. There are still many women who would not speak of their own experiences either as victims or perpetrators.

The question confronting women theologians in Africa is how can discussions on culture be incorporated in our communities so that women find it safe to speak about issues that harm their well-being? Such a question arises out of the biblical conviction that men and women are created in God's image and that alone demands that they live in dignity. African women theologians who have encountered feminist analysis do not quickly jump to condemn women for being custodians of dehumanizing cultural practices. It is realized that even women's actions are too deeply rooted in patriarchal socialization and therefore the analysis of women's oppression has to be done in the context of gender analysis.[10] We need to look and see how our societies are organized and how power is used by different groups, men and women, young and old, people of varying economic means, and so on. Who benefits from a particular interpretation of culture and how is the system kept in place?

Gender analysis takes into account ways in which roles, attitudes, values and relationships regarding women and men are constructed by all societies all over the world. The concepts and practices of equality and discrimination determined by social, economic, religious and cultural factors lie at the heart of gender-sensitive perspectives. Theological engagement with gender issues seeks to expose harm and injustices that are in society and are extended to Scripture and the teachings and practices of the Church through culture. Women, as well as men, are made in the divine image of God and therefore any pattern of discrimination, domination or oppression is contrary to God's justice and sovereignty. Inclusiveness is an aspect of the justice of God, which Jesus restored in his concern for those on the fringes. The fact that gender roles differ significantly from one society to another and from one historical period to another, is an indication that they are socially and culturally constructed. For example, among the Maasai of East Africa, construction of

10. For feminists, patriarchy does not just mean the rule of the father, or the rule of males for that matter, but it carries with it connotations of an unjust hierarchical and dualistic ordering of life which discriminates against women. Patriarchy should not be seen as the opposite of matriarchy. For further reading, see Rosemary R. Ruether's article on 'Patriarchy', in Russell and Clarkson (eds.), *Dictionary of Feminist Theologies*, pp. 205-206.

houses is the women's job, while in some other societies, this is mainly the men's job. Yet in other societies, building work is divided into sections and allocated to both women and men. Sometimes, in assigning these roles within the culture, either men or women may be unjustly treated. Today, most women's scholarship globally recognizes this web of oppression which even leads women to oppress other women. Gender analysis seeks to identify such injustices and to suggest a societal correction.

Cultural Hermeneutics as a Key to Reading the Bible in Africa

In 1994, I first clearly saw the need for analyzing culture as a process for seeking out liberation for African women. I made the following preliminary remarks: 'The complexities inherent in cultural debate require space and a safe environment of mutual trust and mutual vulnerability in order for dialogue to take place'; and 'A new aspect of feminist analyses has been brought to theology mainly by studies of women from Africa. This new thing deserves its rightful place in the theological paradigms. It could be called "Cultural Hermeneutics".'[11]

I suggested that cultural hermeneutics is an important first step towards an African women's liberation theology. All questions regarding the welfare and status of women in Africa are explained within the framework of culture. Women cannot inherit land or own property because it is not culturally 'right'. Women may not participate in the leadership because it is culturally the domain of men. Whether the subject is politics, economics, religion or social issues, none of these are safe from the sharp eyes of culture. However, it is not enough simply to analyze culture without reference to the people who maintain the culture and on whom the culture impacts. Here is where the need arises for a gender-sensitive cultural hermeneutics because it doubles in addressing issues of culture while being critical of that culture from a gender perspective.

As a project done within the framework of theological education, this work must also show how the Church is part and parcel of the subject of analysis. It is in the Church that the dilemma of how Africans should live as Christians and cultural people thrives. Since the Bible forms the base and informs the African Christian on what they can validate or not validate in their culture, I will start from the framework of reading the Bible with cultural eyes. I present in this

11.   See the report of the United Nations on the Fourth World Conference on Women, 'Beijing Declaration and the Platform for Action', 1995, United Nations Information Center, New York.

study some of the clues to understanding cultural hermeneutics. I suggest that a cultural hermeneutic is a first step towards a biblical hermeneutic.

I argue that the culture of the reader in Africa has more influence on the way the biblical text is understood and used in communities than the historical culture of the text. By so stating, I suggest that not knowing the nuances of the culture into which the Bible is read or preached has far more wide-reaching repercussions for the exegesis of texts than is often acknowledged by biblical scholars and preachers alike. Cultural hermeneutics is a necessary tool for those who teach homiletics and pastoral work in seminaries and other clergy institutions, and it is a prerequisite to African women's liberation theology. I have discovered this by reading the Bible with communities of African rural women. The lessons from such readings underscored for me the urgency of affirming the concepts of social and cultural hermeneutics so well dealt with by many authors.[12]

As stated above, the African Christian lives in the dilemma of the two-forked paths of gospel and culture. Is there a way out and what are the possible choices out of the dilemma? I contend that we have to analyze both the personal and the communal experiences in religion and culture. This study provides examples of African women's liberation theology, which I would like to name as 'engendered cultural hermeneutics'. It is only one of the first steps on the path of a long journey for African women and the African Church as a whole. It is a journey that could lead towards visioning a new beginning for women in Africa and for the Church in Africa. As stated earlier, it was through reading the Bible with women in my village that I came to the realization of the importance of culture in people's lives and the consequent influence of that culture on the interpretation of the Bible. I stay with the Bible as the source of this study while acknowledging that cultural hermeneutics could also be done from a different beginning.[13]

I have two types of experience that influence my thinking on the question

12. See Norman K. Gottwald and Richard A. Horsley (eds.), *The Bible and Liberation: Political and Social Hermeneutics* (Maryknoll, NY: Orbis Books, 1993); Fernando F. Segovia and Mary Ann Tolbert (eds.), *Readings from this Place: Social Location and Biblical Interpretation in Global Perspectives* (2 vols.; Minneapolis: Fortress Press, 1995); Frederick C. Tiffany and Sharon H. Ringe, *Biblical Interpretation: A Road Map* (Nashville: Abingdon Press, 1996).

13. In her book, *Daughters of Anowa*, Oduyoye presents the best example of engendered cultural hermeneutics available today. She does not use the terminology because her book is about content and starts from analyzing oral literature. This work starts from analyzing the reading of the Bible in a cultural context and seeks to name the theologies of African feminists. The Akan people understand themselves as 'children of Anowa', and women are her 'daughters' (p. 8).

of hermeneutics. For several years, I worked for the Translations Department of the United Bible Societies. My concern then was mainly in biblical exegesis and hermeneutics. My hermeneutics education was highly influenced by reading and talking with scholars of the Bible, theologians and linguists. More recently, I have been serving as a Bible study facilitator with church groups, many of whom have been women. This exposure has brought new insights to me. I have observed communities give their own interpretations to the same texts for which translators and biblical scholars have labored to provide interpretations presumed to be faithful to the meaning of those texts in ancient Palestine. I have noticed that popular Bible readers do not really care what the scholars think. They read the Bible with the eyes of their cultures and they apply a mirror-image reading. Sometimes the Bible helps read their cultures while at other times their culture gives meaning to the texts of the Bible.

For generations, Bible translators promulgated theories which implied that it was possible to translate the texts of the Bible in a manner so faithful to the original that the translator's shadow is completely absent from such trans-lations. This is no longer believed to be the case. Today, Bible translators are content with seeking a certain level of faithful equivalence in meaning and hence the subject of hermeneutics has become very important to Bible trans-lation work. For, indeed, rendering the original words faithful in any receptor language is not a guarantee that the modern readers will understand and assimilate that text in the way in which the original audience did in ancient Palestine. The issue of historical distance from the original is important, but even more so, the culture in which a text is created or read bears a very important role in its hermeneutics.

Background of the Community Studied

John Mbiti has described the African people as 'notoriously religious'.[14] If that is the case, then the women of Africa are doubly notorious. Their religiosity is not shaped by the Church alone, but by all that is part of their social and cultural milieu. African rural people live in communities that do not suffer from consumerism and are not yet culprits of secularization. Instead, their lives are marked by constant struggles and commitment to sustain life in a cultural as well as a religious manner. Reading the Bible with rural women in Africa is a very religious task because the women are a deeply religious people.

---

14.   Conversation in a study team of the Lutheran World Federation, 'African Indigenous Regions', Nairobi, 1994. I believe he was reciting what he has written about in one of his books.

Women whose ideas I describe in this study would be named 'poor' by global economic standards. Yet, they do not name themselves as such. They struggle daily in ways which seem inhuman and altogether unfair. Yet they believe that God is accompanying them in all these. When they till the land with only a small hoe, make several trips to the river to fetch water for family use, search the forests for dry wood for firewood used as cooking fuel, or walk for miles to buy and sell their farm produce, they name God as their most faithful companion. These women are strong and courageous. They give birth to many children in their homes without modern medicine. Their struggle for life without technology has, on the one hand, added the burden of laborious, never-ending fatigue. Yet, on the other hand, it is this lack of technology that keeps consumerism out of rural Africa. Everything is valuable, even an empty plastic bottle, which would normally be garbage in the cities or in the West, is a treasured item in rural Africa.

Rural women of Africa often wage battles with elements of nature: droughts, floods, rains and thunder. Sometimes, the elements of nature win and all of life, including plants, animals and people, are affected. Death in rural African villages is common. People and animals die from illness as well as from natural catastrophes such as thunder, drought, floods or even locust invasion. Children die from malnutrition, malaria, diarrhea, common colds and so many other ailments which no longer afflict the developed countries fatally. Women die from childbirth, other maternal illnesses and from sheer exhaustion. Men, women and children are currently dying from AIDS. Needless to say, men and women in rural villages age very quickly and die. When these traumas happen, they are given a religious interpretation. None of the above is accepted as the real cause of death; there is always something beyond the obvious cause of death. People ask, why did that particular tree fall on that particular person at that particular time and not on any other person? How could malaria pick out my own child out of all the children in this world? Many questions are asked and an equal number of answers are given to explain these happenings. These theological questions and answers are indicative of the people's search for knowledge about the gods or God. Most of the time, the search culminates in indigenous religious atonement and/or Christian prayers. After this, people pick themselves up and begin again. The second time around, they may have a bumper harvest; children may bounce back in health and grow to adulthood. Pregnant mothers and animals may give birth to healthy offspring. Songs are sung, dances are held and hope continues for the continent of Africa that remains a theater of the mysterious for the rest of the world.

It is among such communities that the Church in Africa has its most faith-ful followers: the women. They live out their faith and witness in their families and in their communities in a way that has some marked differences in comparison to urbanized African Christians. Yet, when it comes to culture, they share many similarities with urbanized and highly literate Africans. I will now present in this work a case study that illustrates how culture becomes a meeting point for Africans, regardless of their background.

Chapter Three

Methodology: The Telling of the Story

Contextual Challenges

In this work, I use storytelling as a method of bringing my community along with me in describing our lives together. Storytelling is not something new to our African tradition, especially women's storytelling. What could be new for our churches is to state that our stories are a basis for theology. Indeed, women globally are saying that theology should begin with our stories—what we feel in our society, how we feel about our children, our families, what enrages us, what makes us laugh, what our lives mean to the next neighbor and how we experience God in all these.

Liberation theologies have demystified the study of theology by using story-telling as a method of bringing to the center of theological debate the perspective of the disadvantaged communities. Stories help to make connections between faith and action because they make use of experience and reflection as the intervals of connection. Doing theology in this manner does not simply contribute to the current streams of theological thinking, it also contributes to theology by challenging, rediscovering and renaming the truth that has been hidden or revealed but that has always been present in the essence of God and in the reality of the encounter between God and God's people. Ever since the dawn of theologies of liberation, theology has never been the same again, for theology has been done out of the lives of forgotten people. This new process of doing theology has renamed theology. Theology is no longer only an intellectual exercise, but also the expression of the religious experience of God's people. Every religious experience is by nature inseparable from the life experience of people. The encounter between God and people never happens in a vacuum. Rather, it takes place in a concrete historic and geographical location.

By women telling their day-to-day stories, the Church will be forced to listen to their day-to-day struggles and the ways in which women have maintained their faith in God. The Church will need to come to grips with the fact that 80 per cent of church membership in Africa is made up of women, and that not even five per cent of church leadership is women! However, women's stories must not be told as individual stories of endless suffering. They must be told *collectively* as corporate stories of a community of God's people moving forward in faith and hope in order to bring renewal to the Church of Jesus Christ. In the process of telling stories collectively, they will begin to shape themselves into a body of experiences—a litany that can no longer be denied. The inessential gradually will be sloughed off and patterns of triumph, steadfastness, salvation and liberation will begin to emerge. The stories will become expressions that free and strengthen those who have ears to hear, just as the story of the Hebrews in bondage in Egypt and their deliverance continues to provide hope to generations of Jews and Christians; just as the stories that Jesus told and retold sustained the early Christian community and brought about not only the beginning of the Church universal, but also the hope for eternal life. Is not that a sign that women, too, can help bring hope to the Church in Africa?

In fact, for women in Africa, the call to participate in the mission and witness of the Church cannot be meaningful until the Church hears our cry for liberation. We want to do theology as a means of bringing to the public agenda the troubles of our hearts and the hurt of our bodies. By telling our stories, and reviving those of our foremothers, we will be able to unearth factors that dehumanize women, and call ourselves, our societies and our churches to accountability. The stories of African women unmask sins of oppression and injustice and expose them as collective sins of which the society, Church and especially we the women of Africa must repent and seek forgiveness. We kept quiet for much too long in the face of such injustice.

To do theology in Africa today is to do theology among a people with much suffering. There is so much death on our continent that reality makes a mockery of the bravery of Job, the biblical giant of tribulations. As if illnesses and diseases were not enough, there are successive and simmering wars. Then there are repressive government regimes all over the continent which become obvious to the world only when their actions get global media coverage, such as that on recent atrocious events in Liberia, Somalia, Rwanda, Burundi, the Congo, and the murder of nine Ogoni activists by the Nigerian military regime. Economic struggles exasperated by structural adjustment programs, corrupt leadership and bad management of the national economies all affect women's lives, prompting prayers, liturgies, songs and poems as ways of theologizing on the continent. Many times, our loud lamentations will only be heard as little whimpers. Other times, we simply are unable to cry. We preserve our tears for mourning our dead. In such a difficult context, culture can be seen as the only constant element for communities. Challenging culture amid upheavals is no mean task, yet there is a need to address cultural questions and, when required, to dare to challenge culture.

In pre-independence years, African nationalists sought the re-establishment of coherence and integrity in African life through programs of cultural retrieval. The efforts in literature resulted in works characterized as 'cultural nationalism' which debunked European culture and extolled African traditions. Novelists such as Camara Laye and Chinua Achebe, as well as anthropological and religious theologians paid attention to the wholesome dignity of African traditions and institutions.[1]

At the wake of liberation movements seeking independence from European colonialists, African politicians such as Kwameh Nkrumah of Ghana, Jomo Kenyatta of Kenya and others also claimed cultural identity as a tag for African solidarity as well as uniqueness. The white settlers in South Africa interpreted the cultural uniqueness of Africans as saying that the cultures must develop separately and they introduced the evil system of apartheid whose demolition is marked by the blood of many people. Scholars of African religions stated categorically that there are no boundaries between the sacred and the secular in African cultural and religious life. It was stated over and again that for the African Religion, the 'sacred' and the 'profane' are on the same level of experience and far from being cut from one another.[2]

African theologians of the last three decades, in reaction to the colonial mentality of the Church in its interpretation of Christianity to Africans, posited a theology of inculturation.[3] Inculturation theology attempts to 'Africanize' in the sense of affirming African culture and positing that as the basis for developing African liberation theology.[4] The dominant participants in the theory of inculturation, whether novelists, politicians or theologians, were men and were indeed perceived to be speaking for all African people. In recent years, African women have strongly suggested that liberation theology in Africa can only be credible if it also puts culture to a thorough exegesis. Using their lives as examples, African women question the premises, that celebrate all cultural

1.   See Camara Laye's *The African Child* (London: Fontana, 1959) and Chinua Achebe's *Arrow of God* (London, Heinemann, 1964).

2.   Evans-Pritchard, *Theories of Primitive Religion* , p. 65.

3.   The bibliographies of those books present various aspects of inculturation—such as Maimela 1994, Mugambi 1990, Parrat 1995, Pobee 1979.

4.   See the Bibliography for book resources on African theology of inculturation.

practices regardless of their negative impact on women. 'How can a theology of liberation be based on non-liberating cultural practices?' they ask.[5] As Christian women in Africa we see the need to take responsibility for ourselves to illustrate the consequences of reading the Bible with cultural lenses by bringing our own experiences to bear on the texts of the Bible. In so doing, we address the place of women in the story of faith.

Late in coming to the scene, African women theologians are caught in the dilemma of disagreeing with the wholesome presentation of inculturation as the basis for African liberation theology. While affirming the need for reclaiming culture through the theology of inculturation, we make the claim that inculturation is not sufficient unless the cultures we reclaim are analyzed and are deemed worthy in terms of justice and support for life and the dignity of women is ascertained.

To do such a theology of inculturation from a women's perspective requires that one draws wisdom from the methods used by both African and feminist theologies of liberation. I draw examples from such methods in order to systematize my reflections, but basically I employ an African method of storytelling currently much in use by African women theologians. In using this method, I seek to examine cultural conditioning of African women's thinking in order to discover the rooting of the belief system of which they are also a part. I choose feminist methodology because it challenges cultural socialization by rejecting the assumption that the roles of men and women have been fixed, either by the Creator or culture. In addition, feminist theologians begin from the basis that existing stories, structures and beliefs do not tell the stories of women or that they have distorted the truth about women.

Both feminist and inculturation theologies are contextual. They are involved in the present state of the world and thus adapt a hermeneutical approach to the text. They base their power of analysis on the people's own named experiences. These factors are important for us as women of Africa as we begin to add our experiences to those of Western feminists, African-American 'womanists', Latin American '*mujeristas*', as well as Asian and Latin American women's perspectives in theology. The choice of feminist methodology as a frame of analysis for doing African women's theology is useful because feminist theology has been tested and critiqued by other women and we can learn from its identified weakness.[6]

---

5.   See, for example, in the Bibliography, Mercy Amba Oduyoye, *Hearing and Knowing* (Maryknoll, NY: Orbis Books, 1986) and *Daughters of Anowa*; Oduyoye and Kanyoro (eds.), *The Will to Arise*.

6.   Womanist and *mujerista* theologians have provided the most significant critique to

The issues I address in this work are African; they are both religious and cultural at the same time, but they affect women differently from the way they affect men. Naming the method of doing this kind of theology that analyzes culture as 'cultural hermeneutics' seemed sufficient in 1994.[7] At the present time, I do not see that as a sufficient naming of the struggles of African women. Hence, I have moved on now and I would like to refer to the method of this work as 'engendering cultural hermeneutics' so as to reflect the challenges that African women bring to the theology of inculturation by examining culture with women's eyes. Thus, doing a theology of inculturation from a gender and feminist perspective is a new thing. I would like to name the theology itself as 'engendered cultural hermeneutics'. A method of theology that gives us African women our own voice and space is timely. The result of the personal experience is a creation of new literature in which truths about women of Africa will be told. The new literature from women provides light to new ways of reading the Bible.

African Women Doing Communal Theology

One of the greatest benefits of women's scholarship has been to hear stories of women by women and to become aware that the subordination of women as a gender is a worldwide phenomenon defying the confines of race, class, creed or nationality. This global reality was affirmed at the Fourth World Conference on Women, held in Beijing, 4–15 September 1995. Here it was stated unequivocally that there is not a single state in the world where women are safe from violence or are treated as equals with men.[8] Thus, despite women's diverse social, economic and political backgrounds, by virtue of belonging to the female gender, women constitute an oppressed social group. The social construction of roles and status relegates women to an inferior position. This gender subordination is articulated through various institutions both public and private. The subordination of women has been legitimized throughout history, in literature, art and folk stories told from one generation to the next. The socialization of all people, men and women alike, has continued to propagate the myth that women are inferior beings and, in some cases, less than human.

feminist theology. See books such as Ada Maria Isasi-Diaz (1993); Katie G. Cannon (1988); Delores S. Williams (1994).

7.   See Ofelia Ortega, *Women's Visions: Theological Reflection, Celebration, Action* (Geneva: WCC Publications, 1995), pp. 18-25.

8.   See Beijing Declaration and the Platform for Action.

Together with other women, I am a co-founder of the Circle of Concerned African Women Theologians (hereafter, 'the Circle'). The Circle is an organization with a clear vision to encourage African women to write and publish their works. The goal of the Circle is to promote the well-being of African women and all women through theological analysis and the study of the Bible, which commits us to social action. The discovery of women's theology has provided for us a renewal and a reformation not yet realized or acknowledged by the Church. It is a renewal that I wish for all women in Africa and for the whole Church in Africa.

Since its birth in Ghana in 1989, the Circle has provided African women with a safe place to dare speak and write about many subjects considered as 'taboo' in the African culture. The most courageous move has been to talk openly about sexuality. The Circle women are talking about sexuality as much as they are talking about anything else. Bernadette Mbuy Beya, a Roman Catholic religious sister from Congo (former Zaire), reiterates this cultural taboo as she categorically states that:

> The implications of sexuality in our culture make it anything but comfortable for us to address this topic. In our culture, the subject is a taboo. Despite the difficulties, however, some of us African women determined to study this matter in depth. After all, sexuality is a prime factor in the determination of behavioral reality, both of human beings in general and of women in particular.[9]

It is remarkable that in almost all of the writings of the Circle women have something to say on sexuality even if only implicitly between the lines. Sexuality is defined in very broad terms as both an expression of our identity and a means by which we express our relationships with each other in our communities. Thus, for us in Africa, relationships are at the heart of sexuality. Bernadette Mbuy-Beya provides an African definition of sexuality as: 'the ensemble of activities by which human beings seek and attain satisfaction of their sexual inclination... Our traditional behavior and customs include a whole series of sexual initiatory practices...'[10]

She goes on to explore sexuality in categories of marriage, fidelity, prostitution and single life. Other African women address sexuality through discussions on polygamy, clitoridectomy, secret societies, barrenness, child marriages and sex in societies. Behind all of these practices there are certain implications for the sexuality of society.[11]

---

9.   Bernadette Mbuy Beya, 'Human Sexuality, Marriage, and Prostitution', in Oduyoye and Kanyoro (eds.), *The Will to Arise*, p. 155.

10.   Mbuy Beya, 'Human Sexuality', p. 156.

11.   Mbuy Beya, 'Human Sexuality', p. 155-57.

I have singled out sexuality because it is the foundation for engendering cultural hermeneutics. Many cultural behaviors that are detrimental to women's health are closely linked to sexuality. Sexuality and fertility are one issue. A whole string of factors are attached to fertility such as value for children, impact of AIDS, female circumcision, polygamy. Many women in Africa testify to the Churches' fears and suspicions of 'women's sexuality'. Sexuality is given as an excuse for denying ordination to women. Not only are women's bodies seen as symbols of sexuality, but also, and because of that, women are seen to be unacceptable for church leadership. It is interesting to me that the African society, which is very hospitable to new life, has not provided a theology that affirms the woman through whom new life finds a possibility for growth.

A Safe Place to Speak for Ourselves

African women have benefited from the global women's theological works and now African women have joined the bandwagon of doing theology. Although not named as feminist theology, African women's theology foremost values the humanity of women as those also created in the image of God. African women's theology roots its relevance in its response to the dilemmas and celebrations of God's people on the African continent. It requires taking the African worldview into account in the analysis. This nevertheless does not mean that there should be an assumption that even the African worldview or feminist view is universal or has only one way of interpretation. Here, I am reminded of the story told by Annelies Knoppers about the development of the Dutch feminist movement:

> In the early years of the Dutch Christian feminist movement, a theology of harmony prevailed, in which shared meanings were assumed. Yet Christian feminists are part of a society in which various forms of power inequality are deeply embedded. Consequently, they, too, tend to have internalized 'isms', such as racism, and sexism and they may have privileges based on their skin color, sexual preference and/or class. Most feminists have therefore rejected the idea of 'sisterhood is global'. Yet many also recognize that, separatism based on a form or forms of oppression has its place, our struggle against oppression can be strengthened when we bundle our perspectives and our strengths. Thus, striving for 'community' within the context of difference in social power continues. Yet, even here questions arise: What does community mean? Whose definition prevails? Currently the Dutch Christian feminist movement is exploring the possibility of community, given the diversity of its members.[12]

12. Extract from unpublished article by Annelies Knoppers, 'Towards Creating

Often times, detractors choose to perceive the efforts of African women as foreign and Western and not conversant with our African values and religious beliefs, especially when we struggle to be honest with our differences. Such people tell African women theologians to be silent and submissive in the face of injustice and oppression. They condemn us when we do not sing in unison on all issues affecting women. Difference of opinion among women on any issue is capitalized on for criticism. This kind of feedback takes its toll on women and threatens many who genuinely seek the way of justice. To choose to move forward despite the criticisms is a privilege of only a few who have other support systems such as understanding families or economic and social self-reliance. This already defines the social location of those women who chose to actively protest the status of women either through theology, the legal systems, political activism or any other means possible. Christian women activists in Africa are engaged in doing a theology which seeks to find the link between the level of grace, where men and women are considered equal before God, and Christian anthropology, establishing relationships between God and the people. Richard Cunningham captures this well for me when he describes theology as 'an ongoing conversation of the saints between the faith once-given and the real life of specific human communities. Christian theology is an activity, not a system.'[13]

Another method employed by this study and used significantly by other African theologians is talking with other women theologians and orally testing out the things we hear.[14] Doing theology in Africa today has to take into account the rural non-literate women. This is a question of method not content. Many women on our continent cannot read and write but they sing, they dance and they speak. However, when it comes to the written Scriptures as the basis for belief, they will always depend on other people interpreting the Scriptures for them. Thus, the image of who they are in the story of faith largely depends on the teaching they receive.

For a long time, print media have marginalized the voices of African women. African rural women are singing songs; they are creating poetry, proverbs and dirges. Their reflections should challenge us to do theology in a different way.

"Community" in the Context of Difference', Kerk en Wereld, Stichting Oecumenische Vrouwensynode, Postbus 19, 3970, AA, Driebergen, Netherlands.

13.   See, Richard Cunningham 'Theologizing in a Global Context: Changing Contours', *Review and Expositor*, a quarterly Baptist theological journal, 94.3, pp. 51-62.

14.   Different sections of this volume have been read by members of the Circle of Concerned African Women. I particularly benefited from comments by Musa W. Dube (Botswana), Nyambura Njoroge (Kenya), and Mercy Oduyoye (Ghana).

We who can write must explore new areas and new avenues for the works of our sisters to be heard beyond the ridges of our borders. We must not repeat the theft of other researchers who have often taken these works without crediting the original owners. The method of sitting in comfortable offices, producing complete manuscripts in dominant languages will leave out so many of our own sisters from participating in the theological reflection. When we African women cry for inclusion and participation, we cannot at the same time opt for individualistic struggle. Our success depends entirely on our ability to make our theology a communal theology. While maintaining global sisterhood with other women, we must seek to establish our own methodology. The illiteracy on our continent will not determine our access to the grace of God, but it has to be a concern of those doing theology in Africa. The project for this work shows that one can work with illiterate communities and that such an inclusion is an issue of justice, not simply a choice.

Finally, we must ask what the consequences of women's perspectives and methods in theology will be for the Church in Africa! I see foremost the possibilities in awakening the Church to the fact that biblical history did not stop at the end of the first century of the Common Era. It is important for the Christian Church in Africa to realize that the power of God, which enabled the Hebrew people to preserve their history by telling stories about their encounters with each other and with God, is the same that led early Christians to tell their stories and by so doing tell the powerful story of Jesus. That same power of God still lives with us for whom the promise of the Holy Spirit was given and fulfilled at Pentecost. In baptism, we reaffirm our faith in God's power as we confess our sins, accept to be washed clean with water and accept the Holy Spirit to direct our lives and witness.

Chapter Four

Research Project: The Story

The Book of Ruth in Women's Theologies

The short story found in the biblical book of Ruth relates the saga of an Israelite family fleeing from their homeplace in Bethlehem due to famine. The man, Elimelech, and his wife, Naomi, and their two sons, Mahlon and Chilion, settle in the neighboring land of the Moabites. The sons marry Moabite women, Ruth and Orpah. After some years, Elimelech dies. Not long thereafter, his two sons also die. The three widows in the story must begin a new life after the deaths of their husbands. Naomi hears that the famine is over in Bethlehem and decides to return to her homeland. Her daughters-in-law plead to accompany her, but she admonishes them to return to their families. Orpah accepts the admonition, and the Bible is silent about what happened to her. Ruth defies Naomi's admonition to return to her people. Ruth's action and confession to completely assimilate to Naomi's culture and religion are the hallmarks of her fame and her words have become a litany of faithfulness. As Ruth said:

> Do not press me to leave you
> Or to turn back from following you!
> Where you go, I will go
> Where you lodge, I will lodge
> Your people shall be my people
> And your God my God
> Where you die I will die
> There I will be buried
> May the Lord do thus and so to me
> And more as well
> If even death parts me from you (Ruth 1.16-17).

Before reporting on the reading of the book of Ruth by the women of Bware, a brief survey of the reading of Ruth by other women is in order. Ruth, the Moabite girl who became the grandmother of David and the ancestor of Jesus, is the main character of the book named after her in the Hebrew Bible. The adventures and relationship of Ruth and Naomi, her mother-in-law, have become one of the favorite stories of all Bible readers, men and women, Jews and Christians alike. Some churches have even incorporated the above words in their marriage liturgies. The story of Ruth and Naomi is widely read and loved the world over. It is often produced as a special portion for women's Bible study groups, and has been the subject of many sermons by both men and women.

Perhaps the most known and studied relationship between two women is that of Ruth and Naomi. They are two women of different ages, different ethnic groups and different circumstances in life, deciding to stay together in time of need. The friendship between them is acclaimed as a sign of solidarity between women, particularly the destitute, as the two widows were indeed. It is also seen as an affirmation of friendship between women of different religious faiths.

Thus the story in the book of Ruth has empowered women of all times everywhere the Bible is read. Women continue to exegete this passage as they emulate the witness Ruth and Naomi left behind. The story has challenged women to intergenerational solidarity. It has inspired women to put into their agendas the concerns of young people, the elderly, widows, single women, displaced persons and poor people. The concerns of people in need have occupied many hours for women in the Church as they have sought to reach out to comfort the sick, visit the prisoners, raise money for mission work and be concerned about the care of children in communities. Church reports since its beginnings tell of the involvement of women in service to needy persons. Such stories speak loudly and sometimes have been the only evidence of the presence of women among the faithful witnesses of the Church universal.

Much as the story in Ruth is loved, it is also a story that tells about the universality of women's subordination and oppression. This fact cannot escape and has not escaped the notice of various readers. The dilemma of the double struggle that women have to wage against both maintaining the patriarchal culture and being the victims of oppression, therein scores the need of a serious consideration of a feminist critique of culture.[1] The book of Ruth is a suitable source of such a critique because it is like a mother hen: it gathers women from

---

1. See bibliography in the contributions in Musimbi R.A. Kanyoro and Wendy Robbins (eds.), *The Power We Celebrate: Women's Stories of Faith and Power* (Geneva: WCC Publishers, 1992); and Musimbi R.A. Kanyoro and Nyambura J. Njoroge (eds.), *Groaning in Faith: Women in the Household of God* (Nairobi: Acton Publishers, 1996).

different traditions, cultures and faiths worldwide under its wings.

Departing from the Hebrew Bible, Jewish women bring to the reading of Ruth their firsthand insights from religious and cultural tradition that Christian women do not claim to have. Jewish feminist theologians have presented the book of Ruth as one full of challenges for the Jews of ancient Palestine as well as the modern Jewish communities. One of the descriptions by Jewish women of what the book is about, says:

> It tells the story of marriage and childbirth, of widowhood and childlessness, from within women's experience. It evokes the experience of mothers and daughters while highlighting the tensions in a mother-in-law's relationship to her daughter-in-law. It focuses on the experience of being the other, the other as a foreigner and the other as a woman.[2]

Another scholar suggests that the book of Ruth challenged the sages to deal with their own ethnic and cultural biases as well as their patriarchal orientations:

> The book of Ruth presented the sages of Midrash and the Talmud with a unique social and religious problem. In the figure of Ruth, they were faced with a Moabite woman, a descendant of a people that the Pentateuch emphatically proscribes from entering the congregation of the Lord (Deut. 23.4-5).[3]

More importantly, Jewish women point out the challenges that the story in Ruth poses to the central event of the Jewish covenant history. For example, one such scholar suggests that:

> If we understand Torah, the gift of God 'who brought you out of the land of Egypt' as directed centrally to the sustenance and liberation from suffering of the… 'stranger, the orphan and the widow', the book of Ruth, the protagonists of which embody all the vulnerable figures speak to the essence of the Torah. Its women characters challenge the Jewish world to live up to the Torah ideals and in so doing make manifest to us the sort of society, what sort of people the Torah is supposed to create.[4]

The story in the book of Ruth remains valid and relevant to present-day Jewish tradition. Judith Plaskow reports that

---

2.   See 'Introduction', in Judith A. Kates and Gail Twersky Reimer (eds.), *Reading Ruth: Contemporary Women Reclaim a Sacred Story* (New York: Ballentine Books, 1994).

3.   See their Leila Leah Brunner, 'The Regime of Modesty: Ruth and the Rabbinic Construction of the Feminine Ideal', in *From Eve to Esther: Rabbinic Reconstruction of Biblical Women* (Louisville, KY: Westminister/John Knox Press, 1994), p. 61.

4.   See Kates and Reimer, 'Introduction', p. xix.

the month of Sivan for example, coming in late spring at the time of the Biblical barley harvests, includes the festival of Shavuot on which the book of Ruth is read. Linking the themes of human fertility and the fertility of the earth is central to Ruth, the ritual for the month celebrates girl's menarche.[5]

These descriptions from Jewish women have similarity with the African interpretation, as we shall see below.

Christian feminists and womanist theologians from the West have capitalized on the relationship between Naomi and Ruth as a model of women's friendship and commitment to each other.[6] Some see this book as a story of God's empowerment of the powerless. Ruth's marriage to Boaz and the consequent birth of a son worthy of seven sons to Naomi is seen by some of these scholars as important because Ruth as a woman gets mentioned in the genealogy that is mainly of men and thus her motherhood is a window through patriarchy. Yet others see courage in the women of Ruth and point to that as a landmark of the book. Others emphasize the friendship of two women of different ages and nationalities as the emblem of women's solidarity with each other. The womanist scholar Renita Weems remarks, 'Their friendship is a welcome contrast to the numerous other stories in the Bible which portray women competing against one another for status, power and men: Hagar and Sarah, Rachel and Leah, Miriam and her sister-in-law, to name a few.'[7] Such theologians see in Ruth a model of women's independence, solidarity and commitment to each other. Thus, the book of Ruth is liberating for them.

Western women are aware of and have often critiqued the cultures of ancient Palestine for making women powerless when not attached to male relatives such as fathers, brothers, uncles and husbands.[8] However, some of the issues at stake in the book of Ruth are no longer practised in modern Western cultures, and they are perceived as matters of ancient Palestine. They are read in the past tense; those stories existed in the 'good old Bible' and now those issues are no longer burning for the lives of communities today. They are at best understood as good examples providing lessons for today.

5.   Judith Plaskow, *Standing Again at Sinai: Judaism from a Feminist Perspective* (San Francisco: Harper & Row, 1991), pp. 57-58.

6.   See Alice L. Laffey for feminist analysis of her own, and also a summary of other feminist views, *An Introduction to the Old Testament: A Feminist Perspective* (Philadelphia: Fortress Press, 1988), pp. 205-10. For a womanist example, see Renita Weems, *Just A Sister Away: A Womenist Vision of Women's Relationships in the Bible* (San Diego, CA: Laura Media, 1988).

7.   Weems, *Just a Sister Away*, p. 24.

8.   For instance, see Laffey, *Introduction to the Old Testament*; and Alice Ogden Bellis, *Helpmates, Harlots, and Heroes: Women's Stories in the Hebrew Bible* (Louisville, KY: Westminster/John Knox Press, 1994).

The reading of Ruth presented above is true also to Bware women, but they often identify with it only up to a certain point. Women of Bware reading the Bible confront biblical cultures that may be closer to their own in some aspects than is the contemporary Western culture currently encircling their world. Western feminists and womanists seem to be preoccupied with partici- pants in the book of Ruth as individuals who determine their destinies on their own volition. Such an approach does not offer a critical analysis of the community and role of the community beyond Naomi and Ruth in determin- ing the events in the story. It may well be that this interpretation is suitable for societies in which the individual is a chief actor in her own destiny and has possibilities to make her own choices. Such interpretations do not tell the whole story of African women and other women who come from societies where the individual's decisions are only valid within the context of community.

Africans read Ruth through their cultural lenses in the context where famine, refugee status, tribal/ethnic loyalties, levirate marriages and polygamy are not ancient biblical practices but today's normal realities.[9] African theologians who subscribe to the theology of inculturation would tend to wholeheartedly affirm cultural issues in Ruth. They applaud Ruth for her faithfulness to her mother- in-law and they consider it normal that Elimelech's relative Boaz should care for Naomi and Ruth. They justify the levirate marriage and use the text to enforce widow inheritance, the African form of levirate marriage. They glorify the fact that Ruth gives birth to a son and it is almost seen as the emblem of her true womanhood and the key to her acceptance in her foreign land among the family of her dead husband. They pronounce all cultural practices in Ruth as normal and good and recommend them for emulation by African women. Tokunboh Adeyemo, a Nigerian theologian, urges all African women to be like Ruth, 'a woman of excellence' in faith in God, industriousness, fidelity and moral purity.[10] Thus, the book of Ruth for African theologians, more specifi- cally male theologians, is a perfect enhancement of the theology of incul- turation. It puts no responsibility on males, but underscores the fact that women ought to be good.

Critical African women theologians, on the other hand, stay with the issues in Ruth for much longer, asking questions about the validity of every move of the characters in the book. They question whether the women in the book of

9.   See Michael C. Kirwen, *African Widows* (Maryknoll, NY: Orbis Books, 1979).

10.   Tokunboh Adeyemo, 'A Woman of Excellence', in Judy Mbugwa (ed.), *Our Time Has Come: African Christian Women Address the Issues of Today* (Grand Rapids: Baker Book House, 1994), pp. 17-22.

Ruth are indeed liberated women or victims of culture and whether their solidarity with each other was a result of choice or a prescription of culture. The greatest misfortune for the three widows was the death of their male protectors. Was the move by Naomi to return to Bethlehem liberating? Whom does it liberate and why? Did the women really have the open choices that they are credited with? Did Naomi and Ruth choose each other or did circumstances of vulnerability put them together? Without a husband and sons, what could Naomi have done in Moab? What choices were available to Ruth in staying in Moab? What prompted her decision to go with Naomi? African women want to know what life was like for Naomi, Ruth or Orpah as women in their times. Since the Bible records so little about men's treatment of women, African women wonder if home was 'safe' for them, as they relate the Bible story to the questions of spousal and domestic violence that many women today know first-hand.

In the text, it is Boaz who tells Ruth, 'I will do for you whatever you ask, as all my people in the city know that you are a woman of excellence' (Ruth 3.11). Does this necessarily say that Ruth and Boaz lived happily thereafter? Does giving birth to sons make women's family life full of joy and happiness? Is the birth of sons the reason upon which women's worth is to be culturally applauded?

African women notice the age difference in the marriage between Boaz and Ruth. The age margin between Ruth and Boaz is an issue of concern when related to child marriages and sexual abuse of women by men in power. How about when such a biblical story is used as a justification also for African families who marry their young girls to old men? Thus these questions, generated by the life experience of African women, pose a dilemma for basing liberation theology on cultural practices that have the potential for denying women possibilities for 'abundant life' (Jn 10.10). How can these practices capture the vision of Jesus who saw his mission:

> To bring good news to the poor
> To proclaim release to the captives
> and recovery of sight to the blind
> And to let the oppressed go free
> And to proclaim the year of the Lord's favor (Lk. 4.18-19).

In interpreting the story of Ruth, we see that the proverbial dilemma of the hyena is the dilemma of African women Bible readers. The aroma of feminist and womanist theology is strong and delicious, but is it worth following all the way when in fact it is evident that African women's experiences are currently missing from the recorded experiences on which it is based? The second fork of the road offers the aroma of African theology of inculturation, but it too does not analyze women's experience in culture. Thus, the use of both feminist and inculturation frameworks still does not include the African women's reality. Although highly influenced by feminist-critical methods used by women globally, the African women differ significantly from Western feminist and womanist theologians whose hermeneutics are highly dependent on individual experiences and are void of the experiences of the communal living of Africa. Feminist and womanist hermeneutics do not share the cultural heritage of Africa which African women share in common with African men. African women therefore find themselves at a crossroads with womanist and feminist theologies that are not inculturated and an African theology of inculturation that is not gender sensitive. Thus, neither feminist, womanist nor inculturation theology offers a liberating theology for African women. There has to be a turning point, and that can only happen if African women make the decision on whether to remain with our legs torn apart at this forked path or decide not to follow the aroma of somebody else's meat. Can we create our own feast and stop snooping in other people's delicacies? Perhaps we can. *A more promising approach must take into account the hermeneutics of the African culture and the engendering culture both at the same time.* The Bible study with the women of Bware provides an example of this alternative approach.

The Festival on Ruth

In August 1996, I was invited by the women in my village to facilitate an ecumenical retreat. It had been organized as one of the follow-up events which arose from the Bible studies we had done together in 1994 when I was in my village for my father's burial. The three-day retreat was attended by 150 rural women of all ages. Normally, these women would always be at home, attending to all household chores, cooking, and caring for people, gardens and animals. They left their routine jobs and came to this 'treat' which turned out to be a theater of cultural and biblical hermeneutics.

The retreat was held at a girls' boarding school. Here, they occupied the premises normally occupied by their children. There were younger women with their children tied on their backs with a *kanga*,[11] accompanied by a young girl to take care of the baby while the mother was in 'class'. Middle-aged

---

11. A *kanga* is a two-meter piece of cloth which women of Africa use for multiple purposes. It ties babies on the back, it is an apron while doing household chores, it can be made into a support ring on which things are carried on the head, etc. Every rural woman will try to own this one piece of cloth and look after it for a long time.

women without babies dominated the group. They symbolized the freedom earned after years of giving birth and raising children. Older women, whose experience of life was witnessed by their walking sticks, punctuated the gathering and were the center of attraction. Younger women always seemed to pose the silent question to them, 'How did you come this far? Teach us!' Age in African culture is not only respected, but it is also extremely revered.

We chose to read the book of Ruth by a democratic majority vote. In a choice of several stories of both the New Testament and the Old Testament, the book of Ruth was the most loved by the women of Bware. Everyone in the group knew something about the story of Ruth even before we started to study it in the workshop. We made decisions together on how we were going to read it. The women gathered for the occasion, divided their tasks among themselves and worked in five groups. Each group was required to bring a report to the plenary in the form of drama, storytelling, mime, song or any other format the particular group found most appropriate. The groups were to be well mixed in so far as literacy and denomination were concerned. Luckily, all the participants spoke the same language, Maragoli (a dialect of Luyia), so that was the language of communication. A decision was made to concentrate our attention mainly on the women characters in the book of Ruth. There is no other way for me to name the reports on these Bible studies than to call them 'a festival on Ruth'. Never before had I seen women read themselves into the Bible as did this group. This report contains only glimpses of samples of what was said and done and they are a limitation of what I was able to capture and translate from recorded tapes, a few notes I was able to take, and my memory and involvement in the process. There is so much that cannot be recaptured since drama cannot be captured except by a moving camera which I regret not to have had.

What, then, does the book of Ruth say to the rural African women of Bware? Does the reading of the book of Ruth have a message for women of different ages in Bware? Is that ancient Hebrew story relevant to their lives as African rural women? How do they read that text? How do they own it? Who are the characters they most identify with and why? What is the message in the book of Ruth for women who see themselves as Naomis (older widow women) or Ruths (mother of sons) or Orpahs (women for whom the community does not sing their chorus by telling their story)? The questions are endless. The context of African women necessitates many questions to Ruth, Naomi and Orpah. For attempting to explore and respond to some of the above questions, the group of 150 women and their children divided themselves into smaller units and the tasks were distributed among them as follows:

Group 1:   A mixed group of younger and older women.
Task: Read the whole book and retell it in a story using their own
            words.

Group 2:   Composed of mainly older women.
Task: Study Naomi and present their interpretation of Naomi.

Group 3:   Composed of mainly younger women.
Task: Study Ruth and present their interpretation of Ruth.

Group 4:   Composed of mainly younger women.
Task: Study Orpah and tell her untold story.

Group 5:   A mixed group of younger and older women.
Task: Retell the story of Ruth and Naomi back in Bethlehem upon
            their return.

For two days, the groups struggled with their tasks to prepare their plenary presentations. This mode was only punctuated with morning and evening worship, as well as one lecture in the morning and one in the afternoon, all of which were an hour. As I observed, I saw women visiting the bush, collecting dry wood, picking tiny pieces of dry grass, hesitating in their next actions, and it was clear that something was going on. I saw processions walking the road. I heard singing. I heard laughter and at times funeral dirges being sung. Often, members of a group would sit for hours talking, arguing, reading the text loudly with others interrupting with a suggestion or a new revelation.

I was not assigned a group, but rather placed at a central place to act as a consultant for all groups. I had gathered all my Bible commentaries, dictionaries and any other tools of learning that I thought I needed to consult if and when questions came to me. Yes, questions were referred to me very often, but they were not textual questions. Nobody said to me, 'What does this text mean?' or 'How was this in the original language or culture?' *Unlike Bible translators, these particular people felt that they understood the text, that it was written for them here and now.* Instead, they asked many contextual and cultural questions.

The fear of the Church was most evident. The Church has succeeded in teaching that the Bible is without error and every word in the Bible is holy, true and authoritative to all people at all times. Some of the women believed that God wrote the Bible and drew their evidence from the Exodus story of Moses receiving the tablet from heaven (Exod. 19–20). Many women asked me whether they would be penalized by the Church if they were critical of any of the characters in the text. I was asked if using cultural songs to present their reflections would be offensive to the Church since the plenary was going to be in a church space. I was asked whether it would be blasphemy to suggest that polygamy is part of the story of Ruth. Speculation of witchcraft to explain the many deaths in the book also raised concerns upon which I was questioned. My experience for two days was full of wonder and excitement as I realized that a hermeneutical event was taking place among these rural women whom scholars would rarely consult. I waited for the third day, the reporting day, with much expectation.

Reading the Bible as 'Own Text'

The story of Ruth was retold in this way:

> There was famine in the land and people had to migrate to look for food. One of the families, which had moved, was made up of Elimelech (the father), Naomi (the mother) and their two sons, Mahlon and Chilion. They moved from their home in Bethlehem to another place where people called Moabites lived. They were welcomed and given a place to stay and to grow food and settle. They learned the language and customs of the place. They adapted very well and settled, without experiencing any tribal discrimination. Thus, Elimelech and Naomi allowed their sons to marry wives from the tribe of the Moabites. Ruth and Orpah were the wives, but we don't know which one was for Mahlon and which was for Chilion.
>
> But tragedy fell. First Elimelech died. Ten years later, both Mahlon and Chilion died, leaving two young widows, Ruth and Orpah. Perhaps Naomi realized that all these deaths had come to them because they had neglected their own customs and adapted foreign customs. She knew that unless she returned to her land, she would be a cause for more trouble. So, she decided to go back to Bethlehem maybe to offer a sacrifice and ask the elders to cleanse the family. It is quite clear that there was a curse on the family, since Naomi never gave birth to any other children while they were in the Moabite country. Also, their sons were married for ten years and they never left any children. This whole migration was riddled with something evil. Somebody in the family of Elimelech pronounced words of a curse before they left. Maybe the Elimelech family migrated secretly and left others suffering and they did not offer the opportunity of migrating to the others. They left on their own because they had the means and they were being punished for negligence and individualism. Maybe they migrated and did not tell people where they were going and they could have disappeared without paying their debts. If you don't pay what you have borrowed from someone, a curse will follow you wherever you go. Maybe they neglected going back to their home from time to time to pay homage to those who died and the curse of death

wreaked revenge on them. Anyway, these are just our thoughts because all these people could not have just died for nothing. (Recorded in Maragoli and translated by the author.)

Naomi's Tragedy

Another line of thought from the group picked up the theme of famine and the consequent refugee status and presented this in a drama. The actors, who named their play *The Tragedy of Naomi*, began by creating a scene of drought with dry wood and dry grass as they showed the cause of famine in the land of Bethlehem. Real mothers with no food to give their real children on the stage created a terribly sympathetic scene that is so real to the continent of Africa. Without words, they mimed their struggle to survive by looking for wild berries, which were nowhere. They created scenery of extreme drought which was made worse by miming an attack from locusts, eating even the smallest remaining plant. The miserable situation created a dilemma between Naomi and Elimelech. An argument developed. Should they migrate or die together with their children, the future of their clan and family? Should they risk moving to a place far away where people are different? The actors managed to create an agonizing Naomi, resisting the move, yet unable to see a solution to the famine. The actors showed that the couple had to leave in a hurry because of distress and cultural dilemmas. As the actors moved from the stage, transformed into exiled, insecure, unhappy refugees to an unknown land, they left their mark in so far as the hermeneutics of the book of Ruth is concerned.

After dramatizing the events so far, the 15 women came back to the stage and talked about the times they experienced famine and the times in their lives now when they did not have enough food for their families. They completely empathized with Naomi and her family for the famine that led to the migration. They talked about the difficulties of adjusting to a foreign culture, learning a new language and living far from family and friends, without knowing whether you will ever see them again.

The hardest thing for this group was to perform the role of Naomi as a refugee widow. The death of Elimelech meant that Naomi had to fend for herself. While her sons were alive, they took up all the responsibilities of negotiating community deals. When they died, Naomi could no longer manage to live in that community as a woman without male relatives. So, she had to decide to move back. Accordingly, Naomi's return to Bethlehem was not by choice, but by necessity. The group reasoned that it is very difficult for a widow to manage affairs in her married home and worse still if she is in a foreign country. Here, these women differ from all traditions, which say that Naomi went back because she heard the famine was over. The rural women of

Bware claim that Naomi went back because she no longer had any males to support her. It was a cultural dictation and there is no choice in such matters.

Ruth: The Obedient Daughter-in-Law
The groups dealing with Ruth saw her as the obedient and faithful daughter-in-law. Culture in Africa dictates that marriage is forever to a family, not to an individual. Thus, the death of Naomi's son did not invalidate the marriage of her daughters-in-law. Ruth was then seen as the normal woman who does what culture expects of her and becomes blessed. Obedience to culture was explained as leading to goodness while disobedience leads to a curse. Custom and tradition in Africa also stipulate honor and respect and help for older people, be they relatives or not. That Ruth chose to stay with Naomi was as normal to Bware women as are the sunrise and sunset. The main interest for the group was to discover the relationship that might have existed between Ruth and Naomi. They wanted to know why Ruth swears to go wherever Naomi goes and Orpah does not do the same (Ruth 1.16-17).

The group created and dramatized an imaginary situation where Ruth's husband was always absent and therefore Naomi and Ruth spent a lot of time together. When present, he beat Ruth and mistreated her. Ruth had always found refuge in her mother-in-law who was also the only person permitted by culture to admonish her son. In this way, Ruth developed extra confidence and fondness for Naomi. When Naomi decided to return to Bethlehem, Ruth felt the obligation to stand by Naomi because that was where she belonged as a widow of Naomi's son to support old Naomi, not as a choice but as a cultural obligation.

It was interesting that the question of violence against women came into the story. That this reading has not come out of Western or Jewish women, but features in rural African reading can be explained by the fact that Bware women read themselves into the text and it is quite easy for them to transform themselves into the characters in the text and then tell their own story. This is an indication that such violence exists within the cultures from which these women came. It was also interesting that women's solidarity was seen as a reaction to men's violence.

The theme of Ruth as an obedient daughter-in-law became even more pronounced as Naomi instructed Ruth to glean the farm of Boaz and later on to go 'to lie by Boaz's feet' (Ruth 3.1-5). The latter event not only triggered discussion on 'widow inheritance', the African terminology for the Jewish levirate marriages, but also issues of child marriages and polygamy came to the surface. The group dramatized Ruth as a young girl gleaning Boaz's farm. Boaz was perceived as a huge, pot-bellied, old, rich man who came to inspect his workers and noticed Ruth, immediately wanting her for himself. Ruth, a shy young rural woman, is unable to look Boaz in the face—another cultural trait for a good woman. Ruth hesitates to marry Boaz, but the women of Bethlehem and Naomi insist on the marriage. Ruth once again does not have a choice, but must succumb to the cultural expectation as propagated by older women. Ruth's dilemma was shown by pensive quiet silent obedience. She says no words, but does what her mother-in-law asks.

In a discussion that followed after the drama, the women insisted that Boaz must have been a married man who was either widowed or who lived a polygamous life. Using age, wealth and success as indicators of polygamous men, the women reasoned that men bearing those marks are normally married in rural Africa. Marrying off young girls from poor families to rich old men is practiced and therefore this was not seen as strange at all. However, opinions for and against such a practice were voiced in a heated debate. Factors that arise from such child marriages were the subject of contention, some condemning polygamy and child marriages while others justified these as culturally normal. In this discussion, the older and younger women often differed in opinions. The resulting picture was not of solidarity between younger and older women, but of the younger women fearing the older women because of the power invested in older women by culture. The use of culture by older women to silence younger women was evident.

The question of polygamy came alive on stage as the wives of Boaz struggled between themselves, expressing jealousy for each other. In the imagination of drama, even the son of Ruth, Obed, became a favorite of Boaz at the expense of his other sons, thus causing jealousy between the children and between the mothers. A new insight here is that the book of Ruth may not only be about women's happy bonding, as is said by both feminists and womanists from the West. In fact it could be about women's lives trapped in cultures. These cultures have the potential of making women compete with one another and fight each other. If these readers' inclinations were to be right and the story does have a polygamous undertone, then the Ruth story becomes even more complicated for the Church. For these women, there were no doubts because Boaz was a relative of David and David had seduced Bathsheba while he was married. Therefore, the group saw nothing strange in Boaz, a relative of David, wanting to acquire young Ruth.

Orpah: A Woman of Dilemma

The group studying Orpah had nothing but their imagination to assist them. It seems that Orpah presented a problem of interest and therefore the group presented her as a split personality. One interpretation saw Orpah as a normal good girl who obeys her mother-in-law's admonition and returns to her own parents. Others saw her as one who chose to go on her own rather than risk going with Ruth to a foreign people. Very audible opinions were also voiced that there could have been jealousy between Orpah and Ruth depending on how Naomi treated each one of them or what kind of relationship might have existed between Naomi and her two sons. It was also speculated that there might have been obvious and mutual dislike between Orpah and Naomi and Orpah's request to accompany Naomi was only courtesy. When Naomi declined, it saved both Orpah and Naomi a lot of discomfort. With all of the speculations and heated debate about Orpah, no groups of individuals offered a definite answer about where Orpah went when she did not go with Ruth. It was not clear whether she necessarily went to her people or just left on her own to some other place.

Another view from the group speculated that Orpah was a very young and educated woman who did not care for levirate wife inheritance. She wanted to have a life of her own and not be dependent on her mother-in-law. So, she went against the accepted norm of obedience to Naomi or the culture. But she had another problem: her own people did not accept her fully because she had married outside the tribe. So, she never went back to her people, but went on her own.

One woman was given a task to imagine herself as Orpah and tell her story. She acted it in a one-person drama. The actor representing Orpah was a village high school teacher. She came to the stage in modern clothes, looking quite accomplished and confident. As she walked on the stage, others from her group criticized her for being a proud, educated rebel who was self-promoting. Using a narrator in the first person, the storyteller related Orpah's story as follows:

> My name is Orpah. Not many people know me. I was married to one of Naomi's sons. He died only a few years after our marriage. We never had any children. I stayed with Naomi, my mother-in-law, until she decided to go back to Bethlehem. I tried to imagine what life would be like in Bethlehem, but I could not. So when Naomi asked both Ruth and me to stay in Moab, I happily accepted her advice. I stayed here in Moab and began a new life. I married a Moab man and had children but my story does not appear in the Bible because Naomi never came back to visit me.

The crowd from her group called out to her: 'Lies! You were a bad girl!' At first, Orpah (the actor) simply brushed these accusations aside and marched past her accusers. Then, her group disappeared and left her alone. She found herself alone on the stage without her accusers and suddenly she began to cry, looking confused and asking, 'Could they be right? Should I have gone to Bethlehem with Ruth and my mother-in-law Naomi? Should I have gone to my parents?' She began to cry, not being able to decide what to do. Retreating to a corner on the stage all by herself, she recognized a big dilemma. Where could she go?

This dramatization prompted heated discussion on the character of Orpah. The following are some of the random points that were picked from the list of responses recorded on tape:

> The fact that the Bible was silent about Orpah is an indication of what happens to women who break with culture. Orpah is a woman who has the courage to be different which is only possible if you have money of your own. Ruth followed the culture, but Orpah was rebellious. Orpah's own parents could have refused to take her back. We can never tell what her life was like because there are no other women like her in the Bible. Why did the Bible not tell the story of Orpah? What exactly happened to her? How did she survive? Did she remarry? Could she have become a prostitute because of the stigma of an earlier marriage? Did her people accept her or scorn her for having married a stranger before? Was she right or wrong in not going with Naomi? Orpah is a big a question mark! She remains a dilemma to us.

The younger women dominated the discussions. After these questions were posed, the younger women began to tell stories of women who had tried to reject some of the cultural expectations and the problems they faced. Levirate marriages were the main focus here and how difficult it was for younger women who did not want to comply with them. Some claimed that the community would force any woman who tried to refuse to conform and that they would isolate her. The professional women such as teachers, nurses and community workers who were part of the group insisted that it was better to rebel than do what you did not want to do just because of culture.

The question of whether a woman who goes against culture can survive in Africa resurfaced in connection with AIDS and income for sugarcane. A nurse in the group asked loudly whether any woman in the room would say no to her husband for sex if she knew that he had AIDS. Then a community worker in the group asked if any of the women would claim the right of joint ownership on a family farm. Again, a long discussion followed, during which one old woman in her seventies stood up and, waving her walking stick, told the others that our culture has defined what a woman should do and own and what a man should do and own. A woman who desires to own a farm is wishing her husband dead. Everyone was quiet, no one daring to challenge her, not only because of her age, but also because she had used a deadly weapon in defense of her case: culture. By implying that to do something outside the norm of culture is to invite death, she silenced all. Culture is the best weapon for silencing African women.

Naomi and Ruth: Victims of Patriarchy

The group reconstructed the story of Naomi and Ruth as follows:

> After the death of her husband and sons, Naomi decided to return to her own community in Bethlehem. Naomi was retracing her roots in order to break the vicious circle of the curse. She does not want to take her foreign daughters-in-law, but Ruth insisted and swore to be faithful, even to Naomi's God. So, Naomi agreed to take her along. Naomi and Ruth were immediately blessed when they returned to being faithful to the culture of Elimelech's clan. The women of Bethlehem welcomed Naomi and advised her on how best to resettle. In Bethlehem, Ruth was obedient to Naomi. She did all the things that Naomi told her to do and that is why she was blessed with a son.
>
> By the customs of Naomi's land, Ruth was to be inherited by the next of kin, who happened to be a poor man. Maybe Naomi did not want to be poor anymore and that is why she worked out a strategy to make Boaz marry Ruth. It seems as if Boaz tricked the poorer man who was the right one to inherit Ruth. Boaz seems to have been a clever rich man. It is often the case that rich people can get anything. Ruth may have married Boaz because he was rich and would support both Ruth and Naomi. It can also be probable that Ruth, as a foreign woman, would not have been easily accepted in the community if she was not attached to a powerful rich man. Ruth may have been happy to marry Boaz for security, too.
>
> But it worries us that Boaz called Ruth his daughter and then went to bed with her. This seemed wrong to us, because once a grown up calls a young person 'daughter', a kin's relationship has been established which prohibits sexual relations. How do we explain this Bible text? Then Boaz said to Ruth, 'Now listen my daughter, do not go to glean in another field or leave this one, but keep close to my young women' (Ruth 2.8).

Group Debriefing on the Festival on Ruth

After all groups had reported, I facilitated the group debriefing that follows (in each answer I give a sample of the various replies):

Q. We have spent three days working on the book of Ruth from the Bible. What is the book all about?

A. The book of Ruth is about problems of becoming refugees. It is also about the consequences of forgetting your own customs and practicing other people's customs. It is also about the problems of widows, when they have to fend for themselves. It is about the tragedy and sorrows of a woman who loses her husband and her only two sons. It is about accepting other tribes, because the Elimelech family was accepted by the Moabites and Ruth was accepted by Naomi's people in Bethlehem. It is about inter-tribal marriages. It is about wives inheritance because Naomi told her daughters-in-laws that if she had other sons they would have inherited them and Boaz inherited Ruth. It is about a responsible mother-in-law, Naomi who took the responsibility to trace the journey back to Bethlehem and make right the things that had gone wrong. It is about Naomi's decisions: Naomi, although a lone widow, made the decision to return to Bethlehem and to take along with her Ruth and she commanded all the things that Ruth did in Bethlehem. It is about obedience and rebellion: Ruth decided to go along with Naomi to Bethlehem, and Orpah decided to stay.

Q. Can you mention some of the things which we said or acted in the drama which are not written in the Bible?

A. That locusts and drought were the cause of famine in Bethlehem. That Elimelech's family had a hard time deciding to immigrate; that Ruth's husband was a violent man; that Naomi was a good mother-in-law to Ruth when she had problems; that Orpah happily chose to stay in Moab. Nothing we said about Orpah is in the text. Boaz was a polygamous man. Ruth married Boaz instead of the other relative because Boaz was rich.

Q. Where did we get the information we used to tell the things which are not in the Bible text?

A. We imagined. We created them. We discussed among ourselves. We got them from our own societies. We got them from our own cultures.

Q. Is there anyone in the room who feels confused in identifying what is in the Bible and what is not in the Bible?

A. [Many hands were raised up.]

Q. How do you feel about what we did for these three days?

A. It was most interesting; we should do it again. It was not like doing a Bible study; it was like children's games. It was very nice to discuss with others. I will never forget the story of Ruth again.

And particularly disapproving:

It is dangerous to do this kind of Bible study because it is not spiritual. What did we learn? Nothing, we just played like silly little children. We need to get a pastor to teach us the Bible.

Q. No one mentioned God in the group reports. Is God in the book of Ruth?

A. God is everywhere. God is always there all the time. God is everywhere all the time.

Q. Did you feel God was with you as we did this study?

A. Loud response in union: Yes.

Q. What will you remember most from these three days?

A. The drama, the storytellers, the book of Ruth, Naomi, Ruth, Orpah, Boaz and the stories. The way each group was different from the other. The funny dressing. The actor who was Boaz. The fight between Ruth and her co-wife on the stage. Orpah in her 'fashion show' clothes. The anger of the grandmother (the name of the old woman was mentioned).

Reflection on Experience

I have provided data which illustrate that culture is key to the reading of the book of Ruth by the rural women of Bware. The data have illustrated the choices that influence the decisions on whether the biblical message they read frees them to be human or bonds them to perpetual silence in cultural bondage. I learned many new things through reading the Bible with women in my village. I was gifted with a touch of their hardships, their strength, their hope and their despair. I saw them involved in a give-and-take dialogue with one another on the meaning and therefore the implication of the text of the Bible. Some moments were more give than take and culture was clearly the factor that influenced authority. I saw how and when young women chose to stop the fight and how they regrouped to pick it up on another subject in a rather subtle, but sure way. I learned that they do not strive to save the whole world in one day nor do they work singly to save the world. They work in groups and seek solidarity with one another and when such solidarity is not forthcoming, they sometimes choose to survive rather than save the world. Thus, I learned that 'method' and 'process' for change are as important as the change itself.

It was important for me to note that unlike in the base communities in Latin America which focused on economic and political issues, the incidents that prompted discussions on economics were muzzled by the cultural debate.[12] Here, I refer to the community worker who asked about ownership of sugarcane and the money it yields. She was quickly silenced by the older woman who admonished her that for women to seek such ownership would result in their bringing death to the family. The economic issues were never picked up again, although the smiles and laughter from the younger women implied to me that they did not believe her. There are women who own

12. See Ernesto Cardenal, *The Gospel in Solentiname* (trans. Donald D. Walsh; 4 vols.; Maryknoll, NY: Orbis Books, 1982).

property today and I am sure that the validity of this cultural prohibition is now being questioned.

The experience of reading Ruth in Bware moved me from my original thesis where I claimed that African women were silenced by culture. Yes, they are silenced again and again, but they are not *silent*. They refuse to be silent and that is the hope for women in Africa. I also learned that indeed the Church occupies much of the life of women in Bware, but it does not touch the core of their belief system. The Church holds prayer for new births, conducts baptisms and confirmations for some, administers the Eucharist, oversees marriage and burial ceremonies, but it does not wipe away tears or remove the pain that women carry. The Church performs worship and Bible studies, but it does not touch the depth of women's concerns. The Church only touches the outside of people's lives and the Church has really very little to say to the pain of women of Africa. Gospel and culture are the two faces of the Church, and between the two the Church has decided that gospel is the better one. Yet it is clear that the greatest needs of the community of Bware actually stem from culture. The gospel will only be understood through the eyes of culture.

However, reading the book of Ruth raised so many other new questions for me. Is it only rural women who are caught up in cultural traps? Are men also prone to such traps? How about people with higher education than the women of Bware? The Bware case did not provide any real contentious modern issues of encounter between African culture and the modern African institutions. Even the Church was only mentioned in terms of what could be rejected but not what the institution stands for.

A control situation must be established before going on to discuss pertinent issues that are unearthed by cultural hermeneutics. An ideal case would have been to do a similar Bible study with a community of men to establish if their gender made a difference, but that opportunity was not available. In fact, such a project would not invalidate the way the women of Bware worked with the text of Ruth. It would only show differences and similarities. What is important to making a case for cultural hermeneutics is to establish that cultural issues affect the whole society in Africa. Such a case will validate the statement I made when I equated the importance of culture in African theology to race relations in African-American theology.

With this in mind, and in the same vein of using stories to establish a case for this thesis, I would like to supplement the festival on Ruth with another case study from a secular situation involving mostly male actors but with women present, to see how culture intermingles with gender, education, race and law. What the story below tries to sort out are questions such as whether

Western culture has managed to completely change some institutions such as the legal systems. Does higher education invalidate culture; where men and women are concerned, does the discrimination of women by the use of culture come through clearly or is it imagined?

A 'Dictionary'. S.M. Otieno's: A Parallel Story[13]

Silvano Melea Otieno was a prominent Nairobi lawyer who died in Nairobi, Kenya on 20 December 1986. He was from the ethnic group which neighbors the Logoli group, represented by the community of Bware. His wife, Virginia Edith Wambui, from the Gikuyu ethnic community, wanted to bury Otieno's body at upper Matasia in Maasai land, which is neither her own nor her late husband's clan land. The couple had bought and owned a farm there and Wambui claimed that her husband had indicated that he wanted to be buried in that piece of land. In a controversial and unprecedented court battle which lasted several months, Otieno's kinspeople contested the right of a wife to bury her husband in 'foreign land' whose people's beliefs were contrary to the beliefs and practices of her husband's people. The judge, F.C. Shields, a Kenyan of British origin, using the law and Western thought system in his judgment, argued:

> S.M. Otieno was Luo by tribe, educated in Makerere and India and had a very substantial and varied legal practice in Nairobi. He married the plaintiff, an educated Gikuyu woman and numbered among his clients' people of all tribes and races. He was a metropolitan and a cosmopolitan, and though he undoubtedly honored the traditions of his ancestors, it is hard to envisage such a person as subject to African customary beliefs and in particular to the customs of a rural community.[14]

Judge F.C. Shields concluded that the plaintiff, Otieno's wife, had 'accordingly established a highly persuasive *prima facie* case against the defendants to obtain relief by way of injunction against the defendants to restrain them from removing the body of the deceased or taking possession of it or burying it'.[15]

Otieno's kinspeople immediately disputed this judgment and the matter was moved to a higher court. As the judges of the higher court put it, 'The question that lies at the heart of this matter is whether or not the deceased is

---

13. This case study is used with the courtesy of Dr Aloo Mojola who collected the initial material which he used in his unpublished manuscript, *The Traditional Religious Universe of the Luo of Kenya: A Preliminary Study*, 1994.

14. *Kenya's Unique Burial Saga*, Nairobi National News Papers, 1987, p. 6.

15. *Kenya's Unique Burial Saga*.

subject to the Luo customary law.'[16] The defendants' appeal questioned Judge F.C. Shields's view on three counts, first that it is only the widow who has a right to her husband's body, completely ignoring the claim made to it by his kinspeople; second, that a person's education, marriage, association and professional success are sufficient to take away his 'tribal identity' and that such a person is not governed by or subject to the customary laws, traditions or culture of his people; third, that anyone who marries under the Christian marriage act automatically ceases to be governed by or to be subject to his ethnic customs or laws. An equally important question, which this case was posing connected to the above was the following: In the case of a man and his wife, who is his or her next-of-kin? Western society considers the spouse to be the closest next of kin in a marriage relationship. Many African societies consider the wife to be a foreigner since she does not belong to her married family by birth ties.

For Judge F.C. Shields in the case of S.M. Otieno, it was obviously Otieno's wife who was the closest next-of-kin. For Otieno's kinspeople, it was not so clear. Otieno's wife was not 'traditionally' considered as next-of-kin. A key issue brought out so clearly by this case was the spiritual importance of the ancestral land to the Luo community. For the land of one's ancestors provides the link with one's past and communal identity. Otieno's wife had no connection to the land of his ancestors. In fact, after the death of her husband, her validity, or relationship, depended on whether she had children in that clan and if she was willing to be inherited by the relatives of her dead husband.

In this case, the suggestion by Otieno's wife that her husband had expressed a wish to be buried away from his home was rejected by representatives of the clan. They held that wishes or instructions that did not comply with Luo customs and religious beliefs could not be honored. They maintained that these customs could not be lightly flouted without serious repercussions to the community. The ancestors, the 'living dead', have a stake in the maintenance of these customs. They could haunt the living for going against the customs of the community. Thus, a man named Amos Tago, one of the witnesses, stated that, 'It does not matter whether you are educated or not, you still have to follow these customs and beliefs to avoid ghosts haunting you or calamities befalling you.' Mrs Magdalena Akumu, Otieno's stepmother, who claimed to be a Christian, admitted that Christians recognize these customs in a symbolic way. For example, with regard to the custom of shaving hair after the burial of a dead relative, she said, 'Among Christians, only a little hair is shaved while

16. *Kenya's Unique Burial Saga*, p. 14.

those who are not Christians shave a lot of their hair.'[17] She also admitted belief in spirits and ghosts. Asked whether the ghost of her husband haunted her she answered, 'Since proper burial rites and ceremony was carried out, he will not haunt me. But if as a wife you run away, then he will haunt you.'[18]

Another witness, Mr Johannes Mayamba, who claimed to be a Christian, admitted belief in ghost haunting which required a cleansing ceremony to make the ghost disappear. He cited the case of a Mr. Ofafa who had been haunting his kinspeople.[19] A bishop of an independent church, Bishop Japheth Yahuma, in cross-examination also emphasized the belief in spirits and demons. He held that, 'If you have done something terribly bad then demons will come to you.'[20] Such demons, he added, come as a punishment from God to people who break respected customs. Asked whether customs change from time to time he maintained, 'The world is changing but certain customs which were given to us by God do not change.'[21]

Professor Odera Oruka of the University of Nairobi, who has done research on Luo beliefs and customs, was called to give evidence in support of Otieno's kinspeople. He described a number of Luo beliefs relating to the setting up of a new home and how to tell if the gods and spirits were in favor. He also described customs relating to burial. For example, he reported that if a Luo dies and his body cannot be found or given proper burial, then some object symbolizing his body has to be buried and proper ceremonies carried out. He pointed out that fear of spirits and ghosts reinforces those practices. Asked whether he, as a professor in a national university, believed in the spirits, he responded that he was still looking for a reason why he should not believe in spirits.[22]

There was yet another interesting twist to this court case that makes a case for the African world of culture not wanting to make a distinction between religion and culture. Both parties tried to appeal to the Bible to support their case. Wambui's lawyer argued that Luo customs were 'primitive', inconsistent with 'civilized values', and 'repugnant to justice and modality'. He held that Luo rituals 'are unChristian practices. They have been condemned by Christians.'[23] On the other hand, the lawyer for Otieno's brother and his clan

---

17. *Kenya's Unique Burial Saga*, p. 68.
18. *Kenya's Unique Burial Saga*, p. 68.
19. *Kenya's Unique Burial Saga*, p. 70.
20. *Kenya's Unique Burial Saga*, p. 73.
21. *Kenya's Unique Burial Saga*, p. 74.
22. *Kenya's Unique Burial Saga*, p. 81.
23. *Kenya's Unique Burial Saga*, p. 88.

stated that these customs were beautiful. He argued that 'Christianity is not against culture.'[24] He used the Bible to show the importance of ancestral land, citing the case of Joseph's bones being taken for burial from Egypt to Canaan. He cited the book of Ruth to show the similarity between levirate marriage customs in the Bible and in Luo tradition. It was further claimed that most of Otieno's clanspeople were Christians but respected Luo customs.[25]

In the final judgment, the case was taken to the highest judicial court in Kenya. There it was decided that Mr Silvano Melea Otieno's body should be buried at his ancestral home, after the judges had decided that he was subject to Luo customary law and religion and the whole clan had the right to decide on the details of disposing of his remains. There was jubilation and celebration among many Kenyans. This case illustrates very succinctly the continuing influence today of culture on the present generation, even on many who claim to be Christian or Western-educated. It highlights the continuing beliefs in spirits, demons, ghosts and in witchcraft generally. It demonstrates the continuing centrality of the community spirit as opposed to the individualistic spirit. It underscores the conflict between the city and its values and the rural community and its values. This case has become a classic in Kenyan law.

Although there were traces of 'tribally' motivated sentiments, in reality however, the issues raised by this case were more fundamental. They included issues of Western culture versus African culture. The Kenyan judge of British origin was highly criticized throughout the media by Africa for trying to impose his culture on African culture. The African advocate who represented Wambui was criticized for not being courageous enough to defend the men's role in determining things cultural. In fact, he lost many of his clients. Wambui was criticized for crossing into a man's world by claiming the right to bury her husband. More than that, she had overstepped the religious aspects attached to ancestral land and clan ties, which do not end even in death.

The Otieno story carries with it all the issues that were present in the interpretations that the women of Bware gave to the book of Ruth. The explanations given by Bware women for the causes of death in the family of Naomi are exactly similar to the ones cited by the witnesses in the case for Otieno. Similarly, from the vulnerability of death, all kinds of things connecting our world with the cosmos arose both in the Otieno case and the exegesis of Ruth by Bware women. Both the Otieno court case and the Bible study on Ruth by Bware women raise the question of whether African culture can be analyzed

---

24. *Kenya's Unique Burial Saga*, p. 88.
25. *Kenya's Unique Burial Saga*, p. 92.

by Western methods and tools. If the law did not protect Wambui from culture, can the Bible or Church protect African women from culture?

Cultural Hermeneutics: A Key to African Women's Liberation
The reading of Ruth was a good opportunity for listening in to the concerns of Bware women which in a way are concerns of the continent. The hermeneutics of Ruth by the Bware women clearly indicated that their definition of 'taboos', that is things forbidden by culture, had extended to cover things forbidden by the Church. Doing things condemned by the Church, such as using traditional music inside a church building or questioning texts of the Bible, is considered as a taboo in just the same way as breaking any cultural taboo. This project has demonstrated Bible and laws are used as a mirror to culture, and in the understanding of the people the Bible and the legal instruments are only good to the extent that they protect the culture.

I drew examples for illustrating the role of culture in the lives of people from three sample cases, and in all of them the story in the book of Ruth was referred to in some way. The 1994 impromptu groups of women who came to comfort my mother after the death of my father quoted the marriage of Ruth to Boaz to justify child marriages. The witnesses to the court case of S.M. Otieno quoted the marriage of Ruth to Boaz to justify wife inheritance and the African form of levirate marriages. The community of 150 women of Bware who met to study Ruth in 1996 went even deeper in finding evidence from the story of Ruth to provide a mirror to their culture. To name but one example, Ruth and Naomi's relationship was seen to be normal because death in Africa does not end marriage ties. Both Naomi and Ruth belong to the Elimelech family and even after the death of their husbands, they had to trace back those family ties.

The above examples go to show that whether in social, legal or church issues, culture provides a hermeneutical key to their interpretation in the African context. The cases illustrate that culture is the most important authoritative canon to the African worldview and any form of liberation theology will have to come to terms with culture. Here is where cultural hermeneutics becomes imperative. It is essential that African people learn how to question, examine and scrutinize culture. Such a process has a potential of opening the way for a critique of other systems—social, religious, economic and political. The women of Bware need to question why a girl child has to be married to an old widowed man instead of explaining the phenomenon by saying that our culture requires everybody to be married. If they learn to question culture, it might also mean that they can ask a political question such as 'Why are we poor?' and expect a different answer from what they might expect today. If such a question is asked today in Bware, the answer will be 'God made us poor' and they will quickly refer to Scripture—'Blessed are you who are poor, for yours is the kingdom of God' (Lk. 6.20)—and then continue with life as before.

Cultural hermeneutics requires skills for critical contextualization of methods as well as the contents of analysis. Failure to understand and take into account the dynamics of the African world and African methods of solution finding have led to numerous problems including a failure in communication by most modern institutions operating in Africa today. The Church is but one of those institutions which suffers from the neglect of African analysis. For example, when we hear the women of Bware village assume that the death that befell the family of Naomi is due to a bad omen following them in Moab, what influences such hermeneutics? Does not such a reading of the Bible send us to ask more questions about concepts of 'life and death' in African communities? How is life to be sustained in African communities? What is it that gives life in abundance in Africa?

A Ugandan poet, the late Professor Okot P'Bitek, posed the fundamental question, 'What is the concept of "ill-health" to the African in the country-side?'[26] He contended that such a question needed to be posed and studied by medical students if they intended to provide medical help to Africans. What do you do when someone complains of a splitting headache, and adds that his neighbors have bewitched him? Do you simply condemn such a person to damnation by calling him a pagan? How are the cases to be handled of the millions of Africans who believe that they are haunted by the ghosts of their dead relatives? How about millions of others who believe that AIDS is a curse from God which can be cured by sacrifice? It would seem that even though medicine is a modern study for Africans, medical students should turn their attention to the works of the diviners, too, in order to contextualize and understand the psychology of their patients. It is not sufficient for medical schools to carry out only research on the medicines used by the diviners; they must also do serious studies on the African concepts of ill-health, and the study of African religion and culture should be included in the medical curricula.

Okot P'Bitek's focus on the medical profession's imperative to understand the dynamics of the African world could be extended to other institutions and professions, not least the Christian Church. Student pastors and professors of

---

26. Okot P'Bitek, *Africa's Cultural Revolution* (Nairobi: Macmillan, 1973), p. 88.

theology must attempt to explore it if they plan to minister, counsel and teach the Scriptures in Africa. It seems that lawyers and judges cannot be exempted either. They must learn about witchcraft, the vengeance of ghosts and the cult of the ancestors. The study of African religions and cultures and the analysis of culture within various contexts currently does not receive much attention and it ought to be made compulsory at medical schools, legal institutions, seminaries and universities in Africa. More importantly than that, anybody coming into contact with African women, should become well-versed in African religions and cultures because it is the women more than the men who are silenced by these cultures and the Church has no business silencing them too.

The foregoing study has revealed that the dilemma of Africa and African women is highly influenced by the fear of breaking cultural norms. In the fork of the proverbial hyena referred to earlier, Africa has reached the crossroads between an inherited culture and the challenges of modernism. This confusion and dilemma will continue to tear Africa apart. Indeed, the present is a consequence of the past and the future is the result of what is done today. To get out of this estrangement, new interest in and respectable approaches to the study of African religions are needed. This can be done if cultural hermeneutics is given the space and seriousness that it deserves in the disciplines of learning. The number of Africans who in some way are affected by the culture is not negligible. So long as we continue to look at our own heritage as inferior and only to be studied as anthropological curiosity, then we will indeed be torn apart while following someone's else aroma. It is the choice of combining an affirmation of culture and a critique of it that will have the potential to sustain the modern Africa. In this respect, the need arises to examine the ethics of African cultures and religions and to seek to engender such an examination as part of the theological spiral of reflection, action and transformation.

Chapter Five

Cultural Hermeneutics: The Meaning of the Story

Cultural Hermeneutics: A Key to African Women's Liberation.

The centrality of culture to a people's material and spiritual well-being is well illustrated in the foregoing work. The idea has received emphasis in African circles from all that have thought seriously about the state of Africa's societies since the appearance of foreign political, mercantile and religious actors on the African continent. In this work, I have presented the evidence of the central place of culture in Africa from four sources. The main project was the reading of Ruth, but the project has to be seen in the context of the conversations and stories in the introductory chapter where Bible studies other than Ruth were done with groups from the same community. Second, the court case story regarding the death of Judge S.M. Otieno is also source material to compare and contrast encounters of culture with the outside world. I have also referred several times to the work of other African women doing theology through the Circle. When all these data are gathered together a question may be posed: What have we learned about cultural hermeneutics? An attempt to answer calls several things to mind. These can be grouped into three categories, namely: first, the obvious contention between *the past, present and the future as African cultures encounter other cultures*, the ethical questions arising out of that encounter and the resulting moral dilemmas of choices to be made; second, questions of addressing dilemmas of modern impact of individual's rights in societies that have preference for *community over individual choices*; and third, questions of *gender, gospel, culture and church.*

First Cultural Issue: Golden Past, Troubled Present, Uncertain Future
There are many issues currently plaguing Africa which a while ago would have been simply waved away as cultural or religious practices. Tribal or ethnic conflicts and political nepotism, on the one hand, and cultural practices such as

polygamy, widow inheritance and female circumcision, on the other, are but a fraction of the ailments eating away at Africa. Today there is much lamentation and grumbling on the African continent. People lament because they have some knowledge of African traditional morality, which they believe has always ensured the well-being of communities and individuals. Not only are stories told, but also there are still oases of rural life where people support one another and ensure that justice and order are part of their day-to-day reality. Yet, by and large, the rubrics that held the African communities together have been shredded by a money economy, technology, Western culture and, I must add, foreign religions, including Christianity. Traditional morality has been superimposed upon and in certain respects, wiped out by the strong currents of the day and age in which we live.

Contemporary African society is lamenting a moral world fallen apart. The Africans are being torn apart, unable to retreat into the past, yet uncomfortable about the present and uncertain about the future. From a sociopolitical perspective, there are cries for all types of reforms in almost all areas of life. From the religious-cultural perspective, the moral prescriptions of community life are being submerged by history as evidenced by the numerous examples of people who no longer give weight to traditional morality. This is coupled with the dilemma of those who have replaced the cultural religion with the Christian faith. Yet the new faith is like a shoe too big to grow into or too small to render comfort. The reality of events causes a big dilemma for any analysis of African culture and religion. Even in early pre-independence writings, some African novelists were realists enough to have cared to point out real dilemmas of Africa's position vis-à-vis culture and modernization. While admitting the attraction of Africa's golden age, the fact of survival in the modern world cannot be easily brushed, hushed or wished away. Slavery and colonialism propelled Africa into a world of cash economy. Since the achievement of political independence, the far-reaching effects of colonialism have relentlessly created problems manifested in moral chaos, socioeconomic confusion and political instability, manifested in coups, wars, ethnic clashes, insecurity and extreme poverty. The resulting consequences are a moral dilemma for Africans.

Many Africans maintain that the African traditional morality ensured the integrity of the society and individuals. When people lament about the crumbling morals of today, they complain at two levels. The first concerns observable overt actions such as corruption, neglect of children and the aged, theft, robbery, sexual irresponsibility, disregard for authority, disrespect of family and elders and the absence of accountability. The second is about the loss of a holistic religious cosmology. It is argued that in the traditional society even war was never carried out with the intent to massacre. Fighting communities conquered and captured each other, but they did not extinguish each other. Property belonged not to individuals, but to whole communities or families. Therefore, communities ensured discipline in taking care of the property. Accountability in one's behavior, both in personal life and in communal life, was a phenomenon which applied to everybody without exception. Even children were not treated as sinless little angels, but they were tutored to distinguish between right and wrong. The passing on of names, for example, also meant the passing on of the responsibilities of community life.

Sexual behavior, it is argued, was not a reckless pleasure, but a controlled and disciplined affair. In this context, polygamy was understood not as sexual exploitation, but as a culturally sanctioned form of marriage. All those involved, including the wives, the husband, the children and the extended family, were recognized and legitimized by the community. Even in death, the responsibility of the community would not cease. Widows were to be inherited by a male next of kin to the deceased husband to ensure that the bereaved wife was taken care of and would continue to be part of her married family. The community allowed a close relative of a man who could not have children to father children on the latter's behalf. A barren woman or a busy single woman could 'marry' another woman to share children with her.[1]

Rites of passage, such as birthing rites, naming rites, puberty rites, marriage rites and death rites were all performed as affirmation of individuals within a religious and cultural setting. They were seen to be community-building actions and were never publicly perceived to have the intention of diminishing persons. Male and female circumcisions were performed as indicators of passing from one age to the next and not as sexual exploits for one of the sexes. Communities upheld these cultural practices to enhance the well-being of society, even if indeed some members of the society reaped more benefits than others, and some were completely marginalized. The debate was never over who gained from the practices, but, rather, this is the way culture is organized to sanction and enhance community. Cultural practices were like the rituals

---

1.   The women-to-women marriages are well known in many countries of East and West Africa. In Kenya, the a Kamba people have a very established tradition called *maweto*, which is described by Judith Mbula in the unpublished manuscript 'Continuing Elements in African Traditional Religion in Modern Africa: The Case of Maweto Marriages in Ukambani' (University of Nairobi, Department of Philosophy and Religious Studies, 1975). In a San Francisco Theological Seminary Dmin., course in Nairobi, January 1998, two oral presentations were given on this topic, by Helen Mbinda, from the Cameroon, and Ruth Muthei, from Kenyatta University.

and creeds which identified members of the community. These creeds were also the threads that connected people and gave them hope and heritage. In these practices, one found the oral constitution which everyone in the community understood and was committed to be judged by.

Today, many of these practices do not hold water! Not only have they become unstable in the community's adherence to them, but also other ways of analyzing cultural cum religious practices are now challenging the African belief system. Many of the rituals and practices, formerly considered as positive for keeping the community together, are practiced on women. Today, women are questioning the practices and saying no to them. The analysis of the state of the present crisis often lends itself to looking for origins of where things went wrong. During this search for the 'lost glory' many find it necessary or maybe convenient to refer to the colonial and missionary past.

It is argued that during colonization, ethnic diversity was made more complicated by fostering new concepts such as individual education, Christian denominationalism and emphasis on personal achievement. People's identities and loyalties to similar beliefs were shaken by false and imposed administrative borders fixed in Europe for the benefit of the colonial masters. It is therefore argued that the challenges facing Africa today with regard to ethnic pluralism and conflicts are not entirely of an African making. The West has to accept its responsibility, not only with regard to the present errors of sustaining certain unworthy systems, but also in having been part and parcel of demoralizing the Africans under the name of religion and civilization.

It is also argued that the present disorder in the organization of African society can be explained as an erosion of moral standards that held the traditional people together. Modern life has emphasized the acquisition of material goods, individualism, secularization and lack of sensitivity to nature. The demand for capital has created an oppressive and destructive culture, and Africans have lost contact with their traditional culture and its values.

Second Cultural Issue: The Individual and the Community
One of the significant custodians of the African morality was the strong belief that spiritual powers are deeply concerned about the moral conduct of individuals and communities alike. These powers do not hesitate to punish immorality through natural calamity or direct dealings with the offending individual. It was firmly believed that misconduct on the part of human beings would not go unnoticed. The individual and the whole society were at once accountable to the supernatural realities, to society, to the peer group, to the family and to the self. The supernatural forces, such as lightning, floods and

plagues, were widely believed to intervene when rules of natural justice were disobeyed. Individuals who moved property boundaries, those who murdered even secretly, those who told lies or spoke disdainfully about the gods did not escape punishment. These beliefs acted as a restraining force in private and public morality.

In their 'anxiety, piety and racial superiority complex', the early proponents of Christianity first told Africans that all these cultural beliefs and organization of society were heathen and primitive. 'Civilization' was introduced to the 'Dark Continent'. Even a new 'God' was introduced. What does it mean to a people of belief when they can no longer worship the God they know, let alone worship in their own method? The Africans believed in the God of the present, of all times, for everybody and everything. The new Christian faith taught about the God of the future, preoccupied with individuals and who could be interpreted by only a few people. This 'God' is a personal God! Every individual is accountable only to him or herself! God is to be worshiped on special days in special houses. God had mostly foreign representation in terms of people's rituals and symbols. The role of the community, the choice of their own priests and prophets, was thrown in the wastebasket. The rules of account-ability were shifted from community to priest and to a far-away God. Instead of confessing to the community and taking the punishment, people shifted confession to the Church and to God. On account of so-called modernization and Christianization, African people have lost the sense of moral restraint of traditional culture. What is there instead? Chaos. The result is mental and moral confusion. This discussion can go on, but I do not need to labor the point.

Many Africans today have embraced the new religious belief with sincerity and might. However, the depth of the belief is always challenged by circum-stances. In times of real challenges, Christianity is shelved for a bit and then picked up again. In illness and death, the Christian faith is most put to the test. One of the leading experts in the study of African religions, John Mbiti, observes:

> Traditional concepts still form the essential background of many African peoples, though obviously this differs from individual to individual and from place to place. I believe, therefore, that even if the educated African does not subscribe to all the religious and philosophical practices and ideas [of their people], the majority of our people with little or no formal education still hold on to their traditional corpus of beliefs and practices. Anyone familiar with village gossip cannot question this fact; and those who have eyes will also notice evidences of it in the towns and in the cities.[2]

---

2.   John S. Mbiti, *African Religions and Philosophy* (Nairobi: Heinemann Books, 1969), p. 1.

At the present moment, one of the challenges facing Africa is AIDS. There are many for whom this disease is nothing other than God's punishment for the evils done by society. When people understand AIDS in this way, they do not address the scientific facts connected with AIDS, but rather look to culture for answers. Many people in Africa are explaining AIDS as witchcraft or a curse. Although the link between AIDS and sexual behavior is now scientifically well established, still in many parts of Africa a change in sexual behavior does not follow suit. It is difficult to convince society that polygamy or widow inheritance increases the number of sexual partners thus making more people vulnerable to the AIDS infection. At another level, the moral mores that would have restricted sexual behavior have been overtaken by other factors. For economic reasons, some women have no other employment than the sale of sex, something that would have been culturally forbidden. Even those cultural elements that were perceived to be positively valuable are now a liability as far as the spread of HIV is concerned.

Third Cultural Issue: Gender, Gospel, Culture and the Church
The difference of sexes is one that is often lifted up as a problem to many religions and cultures. Through centuries of being made to believe that 'anatomy is destiny', women were for ages treated as incapable of experiencing God on their own.[3] The insensibility of men to the demonization of women in cultures and religions has diverse effects on women. Women are held responsible for all ills of society and yet they remain bereft of power to bring about change. Wanting out of this discrimination, women's limited choices ranged from being completely immersed in their relationship with religion or with the men in their lives, to apathy or rebellion. These choices although providing day-to-day survival to individual women have not demonstrated justice to women as a select group different from men by their anatomy. History seems to imply that most religions are expressions of male cultures that have marginalized women to some extent.

Against this background, women pose new challenges to religions and cultures. Feminist theology challenges Christianity to surrender exclusive claims to truth. Inter-religious dialogues speak of many different ways in which experience of the divine has been localized in human experience and the mutual recognition of these historic-cultural configurations by each other. Feminism speaks of new contexts where the divine needs to be localized, so as

3. The phrase 'anatomy is destiny', appears in Freud's writings on sexuality especially in 'The Tendency to Debasement in Love' (1912), p. 259, and 'Dissolution of the Oedipus Complex' (1924), p. 320; both in *The Penguin Freud Library* (PFL), vii (1912) p. 259 (1924) p. 328.

to rid religions and cultures of pervasive andocentrism.[4] From an androcentric point of view, ideas such as autonomy, participation and power for women are seen as threats because human nature is perceived in the image of the male, with the female as a foreigner craving for admission.

It is not incidental that most theologies of liberation written by men in the past named women and femininity as a problem, but always as a sociological problem that had nothing to do with theology. In Africa, for example, male theologians were active in pointing out the problems that inter-religious issues raised for Africa. They posited inculturation, as the answer to Christian/Western colonization. Yet they were silent on how women are treated in African cultures. Women theologians in Africa, while going along with the inculturation, have added a caution. They want culture to be scrutinized under a strong microscope. They themselves are leading in this venture.[5] African women insist that women's well-being must be viewed as a key theological issue, quite apart from childbearing and nurturing. The oppression of women by culture in practices such as female circumcision, widowhood rites, diminishing single women or barren women, branding of women as witches, gossips, evil eyes and all other creations of differences by cultures must be discussed theologically. African women insist that culture is not static and it, too, has to change for the well-being of women as persons created by God.[6]

Christians cannot think about the gospel apart from its engagement with culture in which that gospel is communicated. The gospel directly engages the lived experience of those whom it addresses. In today's rapidly changing world, however, a variety of factors complicate the issue of communicating the gospel in different cultural situations. The gospel is being witnessed to many more cultures now than ever before. These many cultures are coming into closer contact with one another. Multicultural, multiregional, multi-ethnic and multilingual societies are emerging on an unprecedented scale, heightening questions of cultural identity and creating conflicts among cultures. This sea of many fierce, religio-ethnic struggles creates distrust and even sometimes violence.

4.   See Rosemary Radford Ruether, 'Feminism and Jewish–Christian Dialogue', in John Hick and Paul F. Knitter (eds.), *The Myth of Christian Uniqueness: Towards a Pluralistic Theology of Religions* (Maryknoll, NY: Orbis Books, 1987), p. 143.

5.   As of the end of 1997, there were ten books by the Circle of concerned African women theologians. But the most complete work on the subject is Mercy Amba Oduyoye, *Daughters of Anowa*.

6.   See the treatment of this issue in the article 'Feminist Theology in African Perspective', by Mercy Amba Oduyoye in Gibellini Rosino (eds.), *Paths of African Theology* (London: SCM Press, 1994).

Many people whose cultural identity has not been challenged now find themselves in a minority. Those whose cultures have been suppressed, even under the umbrella of the gospel, are finding new ways to protest against what is seen to be cultural and religious colonization. Marginalized people name their quest for identity as a struggle for justice. The tensions that arise among these different groups in their search for recognition and identity manifest themselves in various ways.

On top of all this, the encroaching secularization, the corrosive globalization and the relentless advance of modernization create uncertainty, fear, mistrust, avoidance of encounter and sometimes conflict and even violence. What can we learn from these situations and from the Bible on how to continue to communicate and proclaim the gospel across boundaries? What can Christians do and what should they not do? Where are the limits of Christian freedom in a world where societies describe themselves with terms such as 'secularized, postmodern, post-Christian, pluralistic', and so on? How does the ambiguity of our times and our cultures shape an understanding of how the Spirit of God is still at work in this, God's world?

Unless the Church changes and opts to hold gospel and culture in tension with one another, the women and men of Africa will continue to have crises of identity. The gospel will only be skin deep, to be discarded at the slightest disturbance. Many African women will continue to die from sexual violence. Mothers will continue to take their daughters to their grandmothers who will perform a clitoridectomy. Young girls will be married to old men. Young boys will continue to be trained as future dictators, rapists, murderers. The society will answer to these evils by saying, 'Boys will be boys; our culture says so.' What can we learn from Rwanda? This is a country which was deemed to be more than 90 per cent Christian and yet, deep down in peoples' hearts, the hatred that was supported by ethnic cultural hatred has resulted in the genocide that has not stopped since 1994.

It is these points of meeting and tension which invite dialogue between African religious cultures and other faiths on the continent of Africa. I am especially concerned about the dialogue between Christianity and African religious cultures. Such an encounter has been dialogical all along, even if this process has not been recognized as such by the Churches. Any encounter between religions or cultures is a meeting of people and when people meet, they dialogue in one form or another. Cultural hermeneutics can also be used as a method of dialogue between Christianity and African religions. I want to further elaborate on this by offering some illustrations for such dialogue.

Cultural Hermeneutics: A Method of Sifting the Usable Culture

Since the basis of African ethics and morality lies in the strong belief in the unity of the cosmos, it allows for choices which are not binary. The foregoing material has in many ways illustrated that not much distinction can be made between the sacred and the secular, between the natural and the supernatural in the African thought system. The community is the space in which religion and culture find their life and expression. Religion and culture determine people's relationships and attitudes. One must always live in fellowship with the family and community. The understanding of life as a gift to the community means that each member of the community is responsible for every other and is obligated to provide for the welfare of the other. It is this sense of community and belonging together that made it possible for members of traditional societies to care for the needy and the vulnerable, including widows, orphans, children and the elderly. Some of this community living has survived the encounters, but it is highly contested. In the Bware community, it was evident that the community still gathers to comfort new widows and to offer their advice. In the Otieno case, a whole clan united to contest the body of a dead member of the community. In the Ruth Bible study, departure from community by the Elimelech family was seen to be a bad thing and only reversed when Ruth returned to that community.

Despite this seemingly holistic notion of religion, it is also a fact that African religions or cultures are neither free from negative practices nor are they immune to external changes. The unity of the community, as well as the power of the community, is one area that continues to be challenged most from the pressure of modernization. Not all factors considered to be good by the community benefit all members of the community. Some members suffer and are marginalized under these systems. At other times, the pressure to adhere to community norms can become as oppressive as it can be helpful. Cases of African families living abroad being forced to undergo cultural practices on returning to their homes, even if they would prefer not to, are common. In the recent past, for example, women have requested asylum in the USA and Europe because of the fear of being subjected to female genital mutilation. In our forums as Africans, we often talk about our own encounters. During one such meeting, an African couple living in France reported that while visiting their home in Africa, they left their two girls in the care of their family members for a few hours and the family members went ahead and circumcised them. A number of cases were reported in Sierra Leone where women refugees were pulled out of the camps and circumcised by the surrounding communities. In Kenya, sporadic cases are reported in local newspapers or on the radio where women who marry into circumcising tribes are cut by force during childbirth. Culture holds communities captive and communities hold individuals captive to the culture. When culture and religion are examined with such microscopic eyes, it raises questions as to how to sift the good from the bad so that we do not run into a case of throwing away the baby with the bath water. A new story will illustrate alternative methods of sifting in cultural hermeneutics.

First Story: Celebrating with the Community
When our son was born, I wanted us to name him Emmanuel, not because he was born during the time of Advent, but rather because I liked the message 'God with us'. The message is for all times. I had another reason. I had come to know, to love and respect Emmanuel, a friend whom I met professionally. At the age of 60 years, he beamed and bounced with life and dignity. His presence and personality never failed to witness Christ. He provided a role model for me.

Soon after the baby was born, one of the first visitors who rushed to see the baby was another dear friend and father-in-law. At the age of 90, his happy face had refused to take on wrinkles. His hands still tended the coffee trees, often pruning them with extreme care. Not a single day were the cattle left unattended from his keen eyes.

At the sight of the baby, his joy knew no bounds. He thanked me endlessly, as if my participation in this marvelous miracle of God's creation had also included determining the birth of a baby boy. He held the baby in his arms, rocking him as he sang praise songs to him and to me. He made loving funny faces to the baby initiating a communication process, which the infant seemed to enjoy. Then he named the baby, calling him by his own name rather than my chosen name, Emmanuel. He begged the baby to urinate or excrete on him as an affirmation of the acceptance of the name. As I observed the old man and the infant lost in each other, I was perplexed, yet happy. My thoughts wondered far and wide. What about Emmanuel, my own desired name? I had before heard many couples of my own generation, education and urbanization express their frustrations by our naming systems. They fretted over a culturally determined system, which they said left no room for free choice.

While I was still pondering on 'Emmanuel', the old man interrupted my thoughts with an exclamation of complete exhilaration. The infant had urinated on him. The confirmation had been made. The child was happy to be named after his grandfather. The old man addressed me, 'You are my mother, our mother! Through you, I now live on. Mother is supreme.' These words, said in our language, brought tears of joy to my eyes. Through the birthing of a baby boy, I found myself being included in my new and married community in a way that I had not yet until then. I now gained a new status, 'The mother of...' From then on, my own name disappeared. I was supposed to be addressed as mother of my son and by extension of my father-in-law, too. I could from then on not only address my father-in-law as my son, but also be allowed to hold certain discussions with him and even to tease him and send him for errands. My father-in-law seemed so peaceful and happy, saying that should death come his way, he was ready to go, because he has been born and will continue to live.

Then the community of relatives began to make their own visits to see the baby. Nobody asked for the name of the baby. Everyone knew that the birth of a first born son is the birth of the old man, my father-in-law. Without asking me any questions, they simply called my son by his grandfather's name as they declared to the baby their own relationship with his grandfather and therefore with him. Some said they were his aunts, grandmothers and, not the least, his wives. It was a feast of words and songs and food.

Second Story: Critiquing the Celebration
I learned many new things through birthing a baby. I learned that fighting all the time, even for a just cause, leaves you exhausted and dead, and one must choose one's fights. Most importantly, I learned that one's dreams only become visions when set within a community; the community helps to envision those dreams and to implement them.

In labor-bed for our second baby, over and over, I knew without any doubt that I was part of the community and there was no room for imagining 'Emmanuella'. If the baby were to be a boy, he would take my father's name; if a daughter, my mother-in-law's name. I regretted the latter's early death. She had died of hemorrhage and miscarriage in pregnancy. I never met her. She died due to 'motherhood', a state which I was now going through! Amid the fear and pain of thinking about her, I also wondered, though, who would shower me with praises if I was to get a daughter.

When the doctor announced that it was a girl, I named her without any hesitation. 'Oh my!' I sighed. My mother-in-law lives on! The news spread in the community, as is usually the case at the birth of any baby. The women of the clan, the sisters of my mother-in-law, aunts and friends all descended on us in masses. They were coming to honor my mother-in-law and fulfill her responsibilities so that she would have no debt wherever she is. Then the men came with equal force led by my father-in-law. They, too, declared their relationship to my late mother-in-law, asking the little girl to recognize that she is 'a daughter of people', meaning, 'she is loved'.

The women friends of my mother-in-law took me in as their friend and offered information to me regarding the life of my mother-in-law. They told me what her likes and dislikes were, what made her laugh and what made her cry. I was supposed to know so that the spirit of another person does not enter into the life of my daughter in disguise. I would have to bring up the girl to live up to the traits of her grandmother. Through this community process, I developed love and respect for my dead mother-in-law whom I had never met. Although she was long dead, I suddenly felt as if I knew her and as if she was really present with us. Through the memory of the community, I some-how became convinced that she still lived and was happy to have my daughter continue this life. I no longer belittle the community's value for children, for they are the paths through which history is told and relationships built.

The birth and naming of my own children gave me new eyes to see my community beliefs and I found it immediately necessary to apply a cultural hermeneutics to this new experience. I began to see how this naming system was not only an oral preservation of family genealogies, but also a method of maintaining the moral cohesion in society. I learned that not everybody is named. People who do not behave well, such as murders, thieves and others considered a nuisance to the community, are not named. Their names must be forgotten as a way of casting away those traits that disturb the well-being of the community.

I also learned the injustice in this community practice. I learned that to be without child is to be considered a lesser person. Without a child, the com-munity suffers. The individual woman without a child also suffers from not fulfilling the expectations of the community. I saw the boy child celebrated much more than the girl child. While I appreciated the joy and celebration, I also clearly saw the need for the liberation that the Christian gospel brings by proclaiming the equality of all people before God. The challenges facing African Christianity involve living faithfully within a culture that tries indeed to accommodate the pain and struggle of being a community, yet needs the love and liberating message of Jesus Christ to fulfill that which human abilities alone cannot do.

Serious reflection on our personal and communal experiences helps us to affirm our worthiness as African communities before God our Creator. In doing so, we cannot tell only the stories of suffering, struggles and failures. We must also tell about the 'good news' that we find in the liberating new experiences of coming to terms with our past and our present as we recall our cultural heritage and reread the Bible with new eyes. We have a unique history and experience of our double heritage. We must write our histories with dignity and respect. To loose sight of the reality of the continued and arising problems in our societies is naive, but to be blind to the strength and celebrations of our religious beliefs, or the inherent goodness in our cultures is to encourage pessimism.

The criterion of relating to experiences is to be able to identify with that experience. 'Mother is supreme' is a common African proverb. But what exactly are some of the experiences that come with this exaltation of motherhood? When I as an African woman affirm the cultural values embedded in motherhood, based on the above experience of the birth of our children, I must remember the story of the women in the book of Ruth who did not have children, or Naomi who lost her children, and Aliviza who was estranged from her husband and own family simply because she did not have children. To be negligent to the injustices that the culture does to barrenness is to accept injustice. The refusal of the culture to accept and accommodate single life is an injustice also. Not to recognize that it is women who are the targets of this injustice is to be insensitive to gender justice. What is required of cultural hermeneutics is to sift the good aspects of culture and religion and affirm them, knowing that there is room to reject what is bad. It is not enough just to know what is harmful to women and their families. Such knowledge has to be translated into programs and projects involving the community to also acquire similar knowledge and work towards change. Similarly, the liberating experience that I found at the birthing and mothering of children is a personal experience which awakened some reflection in me, but which may not be empowering to other women. If I get caught up in the shadow of my celebration, my sense of justice is distorted.

Third Story: Communicating Despite Difference
The Bible and African culture are not one and the same, as the reading of Ruth by Bware women tended to affirm. Usually in African popular thought, people equate the whole Bible with Christianity. Several times, while working on the Old Testament with the community of Bware women, people would ask why David was a polygamous man and yet he was a Christian? In the parts of the tapes recorded but not transcribed and translated for this work, is a conversation about Naomi and Ruth having been good Christian women. When I made an attempt to tell the group that they were not Christians, I saw the shock on their faces that indicated that it was not worth following the

debate at that time. It was fine to let the belief sustain their faith, just as the belief that Jerusalem is in heaven continues to give a lot of hope and good feeling to the Bware community of women. But in thinking about this issue, I must ask what is it that offends my community when one gives an opinion that is different from what is known?

I would like to attempt to explore aspects of gospel and culture using the concept of 'difference' a frame.[7] I am asking the following questions: (1) How is 'difference' a problem to gospel and culture? (2) What options might we consider when dealing with difference? (3) How do we theologize once we recognize difference?[8] Each one of these three questions will be illustrated with a story of an experience of difference which will serve as a dialogue starter.

First Story: Difference: Cultural Christianity or Syncretism?

> When I was born, my grandparents took me outside the house and raised me up to the sky three times (four times for baby-boys), thanking the heavens and the earth for a baby girl. They thanked the sun, the moon and the stars for my birth. They thanked the earth and symbolically watered the soil begging God for rain to enable food to grow so that I may be nourished and grow to be a healthy baby. After this prayer, my own grandmother passed on her name to me. Then, my grandparents returned me to the house, gave me back to my parents and Christian prayers were said. A little later, my family presented me to the Church for baptism where I was also given a church name.[9] My parents told me about baptism, but never about my grandparents' naming ceremony and prayers. I learned about this as a young adult in a private conversation with my grandmother whose name I bear. At that time, I too felt the need to hush up, because I was a member of the Students' Christian Union and an active youth in the Church. In this context, I did not know how to handle these two parallel religious ceremonies, neither did my Christian family or the church. Among African Christians, nobody talked about their own similar experiences.[10]

---

7.   The article, 'Feminism and Jewish—Christian Dialogue', by Rosemary Radford–Ruether, has been my main inspiration for adopting this line of thought.

8.   I borrow these questions from Toinette M. Eugene as one of the panelists to the discussion of 'Appropriation and Reciprocity in Womanist/Mujerista/ Feminist Work', in the 'Women and Religion' Section at the 1991 Annual Meeting of the American Academy of Religion. See Lois K. Daly (ed.), *Feminist Theological Ethics: A Reader* (Louisville, KY: Westminister/John Knox Press, 1994), pp. 88-120.

9.   I have since given up a public use of this church name in honor of my grandmother whose name gives me community connections and an identity with which I am confident.

10.   Background reading material for the Lutheran World Federation Ninth Assembly, 1995.

I began from the above experience in order to ask how we might define syncretism today. I often ask how long African Christians will have to live in this dilemma of identity. Is there no possibility of imagining a cultural Christianity that is truly liberating to every convert? The fear of 'difference' is often fully loaded with a background of superiority complex, which is well cushioned by egoism and unwillingness to explore the possibilities that might be present in the different. The naming of difference reflects this. It is notable, for example, when Christians refer to those who worship God in different ways as 'pagans' or some Christians think they are the Church and everybody else is a 'sect'.[11] The traditional prayers were hushed because those who represented the Church did not present the Christian faith as having the ability to handle difference. The difference in this case was the inclusion of the whole universe in a prayer of thanksgiving for new life. For my people, God is present in the sun, the moon and the stars. God is present in the rain and the plants. This system of belief, the Church said, was heathen. Our form of prayer was pagan. Those who became Christians had to wipe from their memory any possibility that God could be worshiped in a different way, otherwise they would be considered syncretistic and therefore not compatible with Christianity.

The issue of difference makes a number of assumptions that need to be examined. It is usually assumed that the one considered 'different' has something which is 'a problem' that should not be there, and he or she should 'want out' of this problem and can be helped out by those who perceive themselves to be without the problem. Thus, it is assumed that 'difference' is always wrong and should be made right. It is further believed that changing that difference makes the changed person a better person. This was the belief of the nineteenth-century missionaries who in obedience to the Great Commission (Mt. 28.18-20) went out of their way with full commitment to save the pagan savages whether they wanted to be saved or not. It did not occur to the evangelists of the nineteenth century that there might be truth, integrity or value in religious traditions that were different from the way they understood and believed Christianity. Their world was neatly divided into Christians and pagans. Even Jews badly needed to be converted and hence the numerous anti-Semitic attitudes that developed in that era, coming to a climax in the 1930s in Germany. But there are questions today even for the

---

11.   Whites refer to blacks as 'niggers' or heterosexuals refer to homosexuals as 'queer' or 'bent' and so on. See also Audre Lorde, *Sister Outsider: Essays and Speeches* (Freedom: The Crossing Press, 1984), pp. 114-23.

enthusiastic fire-pouring evangelist: Is heaven really reserved only for people who think and behave in a certain uniform way? Are the creeds and Scriptures of the Christian Church the limit for God's grace? Can we today having full knowledge and expanded consciousness of the variety of the religious expressions of the world's people insist on yesterday's limited religious exclusiveness? 'Is the Christian claim to be the one universal faith by which all persons relate authentically to God still credible?'[12]

These questions are not only difficult to answer but more difficult for the institutional church to face. The institutional church is faced with individuals who are nostalgic about the religious past. There are those who believe that they can pin down exactly who God is and what God wants. Such people are unable to accept the possibility that God is a mystery beyond our attempts at manipulation. There are the people who see the church as a preservation society, and thus are content to live as if the present times teach us nothing. The institutional church is in crisis because it is built on the myth of certainty. It must therefore worry about how to deal with seeming hopelessness and relativity that is a result of the uncertainty should it admit that Christianity might, after all, hold only partial truth.

Yet the Church cannot escape the haunting questions, 'How can one talk about Christ in a pluralistic society?' One of the most visible challenges to Christianity today is not the missionized world but the secular society of Europe and North America. A larger group of people living in the originally Christianized world have no roots in past, present or future of these inherent Christian sentiments. These people are struggling to make sense out of their lives through what they do and have here and now. If Christianity is to make sense for them, it will have to be what Paul described as 'all things to all people'.[13] The missionary zeal of the nineteenth century no longer provides the modern evangelist and missionary with the security and luxury of being a sole vendor of truth as it did then.

Within the past two decades, the peoples of the South have found for themselves new ways of talking religion. We have seen the rise and bloom of various theologies and theologizing groups. They have strongly challenged

12. Rosemary Radford Ruether poses this question and discusses it in great detail, concluding that the Christian faith in its universal mission is in crisis. See also Ruether, 'Feminism and Jewish–Christian Dialogue'.
13. See 1 Cor. 9.19-23, where Paul argues that he has to be like every other person in order to be able to be a blessing to them. Jesus was accused for eating with tax-collectors and sinners. He did not at all avoid or condemn those who were different from him. What better model for Christians could there be beyond Jesus the Christ!

their mothers and fathers of faith by discovering that Europe and America are not the cradle of the world. These 'Third World', 'Third Eye' theologies have stated that the West has no right in trying to make carbon copies out of other people in the name of Christian conversion. Resistance from missionized people is sometimes stated as a matter of fact: 'We refuse to serve simply as raw material which others use for their salvation.'[14] At one time this frankness was shocking to traditional missionary agencies and Churches of Europe and America who were not well prepared for the new consciousness of the South and its articulate voicing of this rejection. The issues for today's mission of the Church really hinge around people's search for their difference to be affirmed. This search implies that difference must not always be seen to be a problem and should not be made to be a problem. Difference is a reality and it can be good, it can be creative and parties can be mutually supportive. To affirm difference is to be open to what that difference might bring to relationships, to systems and to structures. It is a continuous search in all persons for what we might become as a result of relating in just ways to each other and to all that is created by God, the creator of difference.

Religious realities, as other realities, are dynamic and responsive to pressures and crises related to a community's survival needs. It is such pressures which act as levers of change in the religious sphere, as well as other spheres. Religious reality has accordingly changed in response to the survival needs of the various historical moments in the life of the African peoples.

Hence, African 'traditional' religion today, while bearing a direct link to the past, has adapted itself out of necessity to present realities. It has had to contend itself with colonial occupation as well as with the onslaught of Christianity and Western culture with its technological artifacts. In addition, it has had to contend with new political realities, the formation of new identities and the interaction with the surrounding cultures and religions. We could accordingly argue for the positive possibility of potential and active syncretism when gospel and culture come in contact with each other at any place and moment in time. This is the reality that needs to be affirmed. Our African liberation depends on our affirmation of a cultural Christianity where we feel at home with the gospel. A casual study of the new 'Independent' or 'African Instituted' Churches reveals that these Christian churches, which draw heavily from the Old Testament, are also deeply rooted in 'traditional' beliefs and practices of African culture.

14. CWME/WCC World Missionary Conference, Bangkok, 1973.

Second Story: Difference: Cultural Plurality
Delores Williams tells this story to illustrate some of the differences between womanist and feminist interpretation of words:

> This story involves me and one of my white feminist friends. We were both graduate students in New York. One day we were walking on 125th street in Harlem. It was spring, a warm day, no need for coats. As we walked down the street, a young black man called to us, 'Hey pretty mammas, you are looking good, looking good!' My friend instantly got angry because she said the young man was a sexist, assigning her to the maternal role women are always expected to fill. But I felt complimented by the young man. So I called back to him: 'Right on brother!' Then I explained to my friend why I was feeling complimented. It was a matter of cultural difference. First of all, I told her, 'It is an ancient folk knowledge in most African American communities that black men love their mother very much. You can talk negatively about their fathers but if you talk negatively about their mothers, you might get into trouble and a lot of pain. When the young man called us mammas, that was a friendly greeting and full of respect. He was telling us we are respectable good looking women. So I felt complimented and responded positively.'[15]

It is imperative that we affirm the plurality in the cultural and theological interpretations of our experiences as people living in the borderlines of religious, cultural, racial and social plurality. All of these things define our social location and how we do theology and what we do in theology. Thus our social standing informs our interpretation of the world and the words. This understanding of plurality anticipates that there will be many theologies just as there are many styles of cooking! Speaking as an African woman with roots in liberation theologies including feminist and womanist theologies, I appreciate the various interpretations of people's liberation that are now available for global sharing. I am, however, beginning to realize that it is not possible simply to repeat what others have said. We must provide a new analysis of the African religious cosmos that will free us from the missionary analysis, which tended to condemn all aspects of African religion. By similar standards, African women cannot just join the chorus of inculturation when in fact such a chorus pays no attention to gender biases.

Women in their search for affirmation have often underlined the principles of equality and reciprocity. Words such as 'partnership', 'community' and 'togetherness' are key to women's conversations. Women are looking for affirmations of difference that will lift oppression not only from women, but

15. See Delores Williams, 'African American Women Develop a New Theological Vision in the "Ecumenical Decade: Churches in Solidarity with Women"', *The Brown Papers* 1.1 (Oct. 1994), pp. 1-2.

also from all oppressed people—poor people, people with disabilities, people without political clout, gay and lesbian people, and so on. *It has to be justice, and not just us.* Pioneer Christian women theologians began to develop a theology of harmony during which 'global sisterhood' was fashioned. It was not long before women realized that the common gender oppression does not necessarily put all women on a par with one another. Difference exists even within people of the same sex or the same color of skin.

In the book *God's Fierce Whimsy*, an exchange of letters between Katie Cannon and Carter Hayward addresses the question, 'Can we be different and not alienated?'[16] The focus is on the race differences between these two American women. They are both well-accomplished professors of theology, and both claim to do theology from a women's perspective. Yet one is black while the other is white. Socio-economically they belong to the middle class. They found that assuming commonality for them leads to false liberalism and such liberalism poses other problems. By pretending we are all the same, someone becomes invisible in the process. Individuals may develop false respect symbolized by the inability to face hard issues, quickly nodding their head on issues by simply gauging political correctness. There is also the danger of patronizing or appropriating the other's identity. In all of these instances, power plays a major role. There is always a relationship of domination and subordination which underlies choices that people make.

Women theologians have come to accept that truth is not the possession of any one person or tradition. Women the world over, using the tools of feminist theology, are struggling to admit and affirm difference. They are attempting to create space for the expression of those differences, as the example from the Netherlands illustrates. Ranjini Rebera, writing from Asia, reiterates, 'To affirm differences and yet be open enough to move on to celebrating our strengths together, is away forward to the establishment of "partnerships of equals".'[17]

Third Story: Difference: The Marginalized—An Issue of Justice

When we come together to celebrate at God's welcome table with our sister and brother outsiders, part of our kitchen table spirituality will be that of worrying with God. Many years ago, I heard Krister Stendahl quote a rabbinical saying that theology is worrying about what God is worrying about when God gets up

16. Mudflower Collective, *God's Fierce Whimsy: Christian Feminism and Theological Education* (New York: Pilgrim Press, 1985).

17. In her book *Affirming Difference, Celebrating Wholeness, A partnership of Equals* (Hong Kong: Christian Conference of Asia, 1995), Ranjini Rebera uses a similar concept as Schüssler Fiorenza uses in *The Discipleship of Equals: A Critical Feminist Ekklesiology of Liberation* (New York: Crossroad, 1995).

in the morning. It would seem, according to Stendahl, that God is worrying about the mending of creation, trying to straighten up the mess so that the groaning creation will be set free. In order to do this, God has to worry about those who have dropped through the 'safety net' of society, about those who are victims of injustice and war, and about the destruction of their bodies, their lives, and the environment in which they live. This worrying with God about the poor, the outcasts and the outsiders of society is a spiritual discipline that is rooted in the gospel accounts of Jesus' own actions and parables about the hospitality of God's household.[18]

Letty Russell in her book, *The Church in the Round* (1993) underscores the fact that the Gospels are shamingly clear about the option and priority of God's justice. It is the poor, the hungry, the sorrowful, the merciful who are blessed. According to the beatitudes as recorded in Lk. 6.20-25 and Mt. 5.3-12, those who see their need for God, those who would otherwise be considered different by the dominant values of societies, are the blessed ones in the reign of God. Today, those who suffer most from difference are the many men, women and children all over the world who know neither shelter, food, security nor self-esteem, women who are violated by culture and religions, gays, lesbians and other persons are often marginalized. Jesus opts for these 'strangers', not because they are more righteous or more sinful, but because they are the ones who help us know when justice is done. These people are the new community in Christ.

The confession of God as sovereign demands not only social responsibility but also a faith conviction. A connection between the worship of God and the ethical responsibilities, of which dealing with difference might be one, must be motivated by belief that God still understands our dilemmas. The jubilee Bible text remind us that God requires us as whole societies, not just individuals to seek and live in just ways. Sharon Ringe says of Leviticus 25, 'The jubilee laws are public, general laws affecting the whole country at once, and not private contracts between creditor and debtor…'[19]

The biblical jubilee was foremost about the restoration of justice. God's intention for the history of Israel was to establish a covenant relationship based on justice. The concept was to be built on a holy and just God requiring similar godlike responses from the worshiping people (Lev. 17–26). God specifically ordered protection for the vulnerable, naming the stranger, the widow, the orphan and the poor (Exod. 23.21-26) The charge was clear, 'You shall not

18. Letty M. Russell, *Church in the Round: Feminist Interpretation of Church* (Louisville, KY: Westminister/John Knox Press, 1993), p. 196.

19. Sharon H. Ringe, *Jesus, Liberation, and the Biblical Jubilee* (Philadelphia: Fortress Press, 1985), pp. 26-27.

pervert justice' (Deut. 16–18). Charging of interest, taking bribes, showing partiality (i.e. discrimination), are some of the named perversions of justice. According to the description of the jubilee year found in Lev. 25.10, every fiftieth year, slaves were to be freed, debts forgiven and land restored to its original families as an expression of justice. The biblical jubilee is based on the assumption that all creation belongs to God and thus God is the only sovereign owner. We hardly take cognizance of this fact, or if we do, we do not find it particularly convincing or palatable. Thus, we have usurped God's sovereignty. The first turning point can only be recognizing the integrity of God's sovereignty. It is extremely hard in our world today to understand God's sovereignty when we seem to be able to make anything we want, including human life! We can travel anywhere or just sit in the comfort of our couches and see the rest of the world while sipping a cup of tea. The differences in our lives even make the recognition of God harder.

To celebrate difference is to celebrate the tremendous power that can be manifested when the Spirit of God descends upon us, allowing the combination of age, wisdom and hope to gather in one place and to speak to the world. To be active for the future, demands vision and hope for what the future will be. Our visions can be shaped by exploring what might be available in structures of mutuality and participation as opposed to those in which a few govern the majority and the resources of the earth are owned and controlled by a few people. Our task can be to transform attitudes, and move from hierarchy to the empowerment of people, especially those with whom we ourselves have a problem with the difference they portray. Our transformed structures must open up for true dialogue on the meaning of partnerships in the dealings we have with each other in religions and in cultures. We must ask, what is it that is important in our belief system that we must reclaim if we have to be rooted in our faith and to actively engage in our own liberation? How can we reclaim these aspects of our religious heritage? What will be the effects of pluralism in our continued development of an African women's theology of liberation? Will the plurality threaten the unity and catholicity of theology in general and our solidarity with other women's theologies in particular? For me, unity does not mean homogeneity, and oneness does not mean sameness. Every people must find its own way of speaking about God and of generating new symbols, concepts and models that are congenial to express their religious vision. Those who have been prevented from participating fully in this myth-and-symbol making process must claim back our right to do so. When we are able to achieve unity in diversity, then we claim to experience God's power and glory present in the community.

Chapter Six

Engendered Cultural Hermeneutics:
The Power of the Story

Accountability: An Issue for the Church in Africa

The Truth and Reconciliation Commission in South Africa is a reminder to the whole continent about accountability for our actions, both past and present.[1] Without accountability we will not be able to leave any heritage for the future of our continent. Yet perhaps when we look at our troubled Africa, imprisoned by wars, debts, famine, corruption, political irresponsibility, held to ransom by disease and poverty, blinded by elitism, tribalism, materialism, illiteracy (the list has no end), we almost see no beginning or end and we begin to worry about setting priorities. Therefore, we wonder within ourselves how individual Christians and the Church in Africa can or should pay attention to women within this set-up in which so much effort is needed just to alleviate human suffering and to improve community life? The hope of Africa is to remember the future. The women of Africa are part of that future. For the churches to become accountable, they must remember to be in solidarity also with the issues that affect the lives of African women on this continent.

Atrocities inflicted on human life and the environment by civil wars in the Great Lakes region, Liberia, Sierra Leone, Somalia, Ethiopia, Eritrea, to name but a few, illustrate the nature and extent of the catastrophe. Protests have been performed for political issues, but one fails to hear similar fire burning for the crimes done against the women of Africa. How long must we wait? The rape cases in the war of the Great Lakes have hardly received any attention either locally or internationally. The daily death of women in childbirth has not made our governments nor the International Monetary Fund change their health policies and give priority to maternal healthcare. The

1. Alex Boraine, *A Country Unmasked, Inside South Africa's Truth and Reconciliation Commission* (Oxford: Oxford University Press, 2000).

frequent threats and death from female circumcision have not made the Church go up in all its force to teach something new about culture and human dignity. African women are silenced daily by health issues, cultural prescriptions, illiteracy and endless chores that make us age before our time.

Yet it is easy to hear our churches say that they are already involved in many good deeds and some of these concern women. The churches have established community centers such as kindergartens, schools and hospitals. Eager to live in obedience to Christ and his life, women in the churches have continually thrown themselves into volunteer-run activities of loving service. Women in churches and in organizations have gathered in the street children, fed the hungry, visited the lonely and the prisoners. Women have given refuge to victims of war and other displaced people and women have tended the sick and dying from the unending wars and disasters in Africa. Women's hearts ache for their children and grandchildren, orphans from war, political prisoners, patients of AIDS and other illnesses. Women have been busy binding wounds, but have not stopped the war. We have prepared bodies for burial, but have not stopped the killing. We have not stopped the rape and molestation of women. We have not stopped violence in the home and general discrimination against girls and women.

The witness of the Church in Africa will not be credible unless the Church takes into account the traumatic situation of the millions of women and the perilous conditions of the outcast of our societies. What meaning can faith have in churches that seek to be liberated without sharing the people's battles with the forces of oppression assaulting their dignity? Asking these questions is part of the methodology of African women's theology. Yet, these questions frighten churches and communities with long-established traditions and practices of injustices to women. They threaten our institutional comfort as churches, our invested privileges, our secure situations and they threaten the security of our judgment of what is right and what is not. But an experience of faith that holds itself aloof from people seeking to escape marginalization poses serious risk to the future of the Church and the Church of the future in Africa. In order to safeguard the prophetic witness of the Church, action is needed now—for justice delayed is justice denied.

There is the risk of facing the different opinions that bear on the understanding of the witness of the Church, especially in regards to the Church's responsibility to women. We must come to accept that even within the Church, opinions will differ. Speaking up calls for credibility of Church leaders in their own personal and public life. If the Christian community in Africa has to be credible in its witness, we must approach the complex situations before us with expertise. The churches have to open up more possibilities for the believers to listen to the many points of view and exercise discipline to acquire understanding of the complex forces at work in modern society. Different options even in the application of cultural values and practices are healthy and right for our continent.

I want to suggest that taking the risk and daring to be a conscience and stimulus for change in the status of women our own societies is a priority churches in Africa should establish. Speaking up on issues that diminish life has been the most difficult part of our self-understanding as individuals and churches. Speaking out is a prophetic task. It involves some very serious risks. In our situation where democracy is thought to be a luxury, speaking up involves foremost risking wrath from the powerful. For me, those who have dared to speak out despite all the risks involved are the prophets that our continent badly needs today. During the WCC Ecumenical Decade, 1988–1998, many women in the churches of Africa spoke up. Some were reprimanded, others excommunicated by the churches and others have lost their positions in the church.[2] I yearn for a time when the men in the churches of Africa will be prophetic about the things that negatively affect the lives of African women.

The status of women within their church is a microcosm of their status within the society of which the church is a part. Even when the rights of women are enshrined in law, custom and tradition, popular attitudes and values lag far behind and continue to oppress women. Sexuality is one area around which many beliefs and attitudes towards women are oppressive. Regrettably, the Church is more often than not a part of this oppressive culture. Even when the Church has the institutions and mechanisms of justice for women, it has few of the practices for there is no space for a democratic expression of women's voices. The Church needs to be constantly reminded of its task. The World Council of Churches' (WCC) Ecumenical Decade of Churches in Solidarity with Women (1988–1998) was such a reminder. Although the experience of the decade was disappointing in that churches failed to initiate programs of empowerment for women, such results only validate the need to constantly hold the Church accountable.[3] It is an urgent

2.   The Reformed Church in Malawi, for example, fired women pastors and penalized Dr Isabel Phiri when the women in the church talked about sexual harassment in the church and society. See Isabel A. Phiri, 'Women, Church and Theological Education,' *Ministerial Formation* 71 (Oct. 1995), pp. 39-43.

3.   See, *Living Letters: A Report of the Visits to the Churches During the Ecumenical Decade of Churches in Solidarity with Women* (Geneva: WCC Publications, 1997).

advocacy task that women make the churches commit themselves to the freedom and wholeness of women. Women of Africa are asking the Church to be credible as we link our theological analysis to cultural hermeneutics. We give credibility to the Church when we make it aware of its own shortcomings and need for repentance.

The notion of women as partners with men in the Church still frightens some among our communities. I remember a meeting I had with clergymen in Soweto, South Africa, in February 1993. These brothers had no problem with using 'partnership', in referring to a marriage relationship, but they found the terminology quite unacceptable in addressing the relationship of women and men in the Church. The fear that in affirming partnership, it will imply women and men sharing in ordained ministry and in leadership was the point at stake.

Presently African women can no longer wait for things to take their natural course. The models of women in the Bible who needed help show us they made a political and faith decision to act in a way in which help would come for them from sources beyond their immediate environment. In listening to many experiences of churchwomen in Africa, I feel that our cry for partnership in the Church is loud and clear. When we are denied partnership, we are denied the opportunity to bring our gifts to the altar to offer to God. Our talents often remain unused for church growth. Women theologians may teach in scholastic institutions or work with secular and para-church organizations, but are often not called upon to be co-ministers in the shaping of theology and mission of the Church. When women ask for *partnership*, what is granted is *paternalism*.

The church leaders from our communities continually heap praises over women with words such as 'women are the backbone of the church'. These paternalistic leaders desire to shield African churchwomen from growing up. They encourage women to continue organizing parallel forums, but they do not listen to the issues that are raised in these forums. They encourage women to be virtuous and to serve as volunteers for the church and to accept and support the status quo. They encourage us to remain children in the understanding of ourselves and our call to participate in God's mission. They do not listen to the chorus of pain and contradictions in the lives of African women. They do not hear the harmony of our lamentation. Our song asks our churches to empower us and to nurture us towards maturity and finally to welcome us as partners in God's mission and ministry. Partnership is rooted in the shared resources of the community. The ministry of the Church in Africa today requires new and more collaborative strength. It is time that our male leaders let go of the heroic image of owning the Church. God does not assign talents according to sex but according to divine will. To ignore this and continue business as usual at a time of crisis is to be bad stewards of God's resources.

Accountability: An Issue for Women in Africa

A revolution is in progress in Africa. African women are refusing to accept this business of 'our culture says so'. It is a revolution of small changes in the midst of ambiguity and struggle. One sees this revolution in secular and church-women's organizations alike. Currently, there are many women organizing to protest against female circumcision, early childhood marriages, food taboos, and all harmful cultural practices. Churchwomen no longer speak only on 'spiritual matters' as the case used to be a few years ago.

Churchwomen of Africa can no longer afford to remain silenced when people are dying, children and women are raped in broad daylight, and young girls are mutilated in the act of female circumcision. How do women in the Church respond faithfully to God in the face of oppression of women? The process of breaking long-held silence is very difficult. It requires a safe place to discover and build solidarity with the others in the community. In Africa, commitment to the change of oppressive systems has to be done within the community, otherwise its validity will be questioned. At this moment in their story, the voices of African women are not yet sufficiently audible. But women are talking, singing and crying out loud for help, and writing. As we find ourselves faced with many challenges, the impact on women is immense. These issues weigh heavily on women who have received theological education. Many simply have no time to sit and write long treatises with footnotes and quotations from a million other scholars. Many cannot take the time for academics. Many have no access to books and libraries, as money is a problem and the theological books are expensive. Those who pass a judgment on African women as a people lacking in theological expression or reflection need to hear and read our *choked silence*. In some instances, the seeming silence may well be a strategized expression of protest. But it may also be an expression of despair, anger, overloaded systems and other circumstances, which continually weigh us down. The reality is that African women live daily in vulnerable situations and whether by talking about it or in silence they are daily struggling to be bigger than reality.

Some women seem quite comfortable in their experience of church and matters of faith in general as things are now. Others seem uncomfortable with the contradictions that their life experiences offer in relation to what the Bible says. A majority may not have the analytical language and method to make connections between the realities of their day-to-day experiences and the religious teaching. Thus, they live dualistic lives where the church and the home are set completely apart. A woman may be experiencing a very violent and abusive relationship in the home, but at the same time be the most faithful to the church even when the church does not stand with her. It seems that the more the suffering, the more the faithfulness.

Among the groups of women often resistant to change are women who belong to the huge denominational uniformed women's organizations and clergy wives. For a long time clergy wives have been the leaders of women. They are often the ones most exposed to international and ecumenical meetings and in some cases they have been the most educated women in the rural church. Women theologians and women clergy are a challenge to the power of clergy wives. Thus, when trained women theologians begin to make connections between what happens at home and in church, with a view to suggesting change in the name of justice, they have to be cautious of disturbing the set order. It takes time to establish trust with other women before beginning to do any advocacy. It would be easier just to do academic theology; that is reading, reflecting and writing. But for us in Africa, it does not matter how much we write of our theology in books, the big test before us is whether we can bring change in our societies. This is a tall order and we agonize about it.

A majority of African Christian women have been raised in very evangelical and conservative churches. We therefore often find ourselves struggling with our history and our present personal change that has developed with theological studies, ecumenical exposure, and encounter with other global women's analysis. Sometimes this crossroad leaves us in great pain as Nyambura Njoroge, reflects in her presentation to the Circle meeting in Nairobi in 1994, 'groaning and languishing in labor pains...but for how long?'[4] Njoroge, a woman pastor raised in a Presbyterian home and church, laments that her training as a pastor never equipped her to deal with social or gender issues. Instead, she was trained to see people as souls without bodies, an aspect that made her ministerial work narrow and limited if not impossible.

Whether in the pews or among theologically trained women, there are only

---

4.   Nyambura Njoroge, 'Groaning and Languishing in Labour Pains: But for How Long Lord?', a paper presented to the Circle of African Women Theologians, Nairobi, Kenya, January 1994 and published in Musimbi R.A. Kanyoro and Nyambura J. Njoroge (eds.), *Groaning in Faith: African Women in the Household of God* (Nairobi: Acton, 1996), pp. 3-15.

a handful that are comfortable with challenging the text of the Bible by applying the hermeneutics of suspicion to the biblical text as theologian Schüssler Fiorenza has suggested in her framework of feminist hermeneutical theory.[5] At this point, one of the immediate tasks before us is to gain confidence to face the dilemmas and contradictions that are part of our history and present. When we advocate for women to be included in the ordained ministries of the churches in Africa, we are hoping that these women pastors will be strong pillars for establishing relationships of trust and mutuality with women in the congregations. We are hoping that women pastors will be willing to talk about the reality of women's experiences in their sermons and therefore be able to make connections between church, home and society. That in itself creates a possibility for women to be included in the telling of the story of faith to the community of faith. We also trust that the body language of women and men working together in ministry will be a gesture of men and women sharing leadership and responsibility. Such a possibility can have a far-reaching impact in other areas, including the home. However, we have come to realize that it is not enough to have trained and ordained women: the kind of training is even more important if change is to come to our societies.

The African continent's history of colonialism and Western imperialism causes a dilemma for African women theologians and activists at large. There is always a struggle with how to relate to Western culture, indigenous culture and religious culture, coupled with the daily need to support life against all odds. The quest for justice for women is trivialized in favor of 'larger' issues such as national liberation, famine, disease, war, poverty and so on. Acts of individual resistance to injustice and inequality in the Church are seen as immoral rather than scriptural. Analytical women are accused of being in pursuit of Western ideals of feminist liberation rather than African and Christian ones. This often leaves women vulnerable.

There are also many issues on which women do not agree. We especially are at odds on issues concerning culture. For instance, there are myriad differences on how to regard cultural practices such as female circumcision (genital mutilation), *lobola* (dowry), polygamy, the dominantly male inheritance of land, and numerous other practices. Some perceive these practices as the essence of our culture, and therefore the center of our identity. In other words, some believe that these practices help to undergird who we are and therefore they give us a base and a uniform community. Yet for some among

5. Elisabeth Schüssler Fiorenza, *Bread Not Stone: The Challenge of Feminist Biblical Interpretation* (Boston: Beacon Press, 1985), pp. 15-21, 108, 148.

us, these practices are acts of injustice to women and they need to change. The practices are harmful, oppressive and they reduce women to mere instruments of men and culture in general. The lack of unanimous agreement on these issues continues to divide us but the diversity of opinion will never again silence the women of Africa.

Take the question of polygamy. Here the Church, too, has caught itself in a dilemma. Until recently, the subject of polygamy has appeared in Christian debates mainly as a moral issue relating to marriage. Convinced that the Scriptures advocate for monogamy through texts such as the creation of Adam and Eve (Gen. 2.23-24), the Christian Church had taken pains to condemn those cultures in which polygamy is an accepted form of matrimony. Considering polygamy as immoral, and all those involved in it as sinners, the Church proceeded not to accept as members men, women and children in polygamous families. Often, men were asked to choose one wife and to leave the others in order to be accepted in the Church. The Church also found reasons to be at odds with Islam, which legally stipulates up to a maximum of four wives to a man. Recent studies by women look at polygamy as an institution oppressive to women.[6] Polygamy thrives in patriarchal cultures, which believe in the superiority of male persons. Men may own not only property, but women and their productive powers as well. Polygamy has tended to exploit women and children's labor because polygamy is justified as a means of enhancing productivity of property for the man. Polygamy also depicts women as weak and needing the constant protection of men. It reduces women's ability to cope with circumstances of their body such as barrenness. Both in the Bible and in cultures, women who do not give birth or who give birth only to girl children are diminished and find themselves perpetuating polygamy.

The Church is often in a dilemma with polygamy because on the one hand it finds evidence in the Scriptures that seems to advocate monogamy, and yet on the other there is no direct condemnation of polygamy. African feminists argue that the case for monogamy should be based on the dignity of women, rather than on moral judgments or the justification of one form of marriage

---

6.   See Judith Mbula Bahemuka, 'Social Changes and Women's Attitudes toward Marriage in East Africa', pp. 119-34; Anne Nasimiyu-Wasike, 'Polygamy: A Feminist Critique', pp. 101-118; Musimbi R.A. Kanyoro, 'Interpreting Old Testament Polygamy through African Eyes', pp. 87-100; Lloyda Fanusie, 'Sexuality and Women in African Culture', pp. 134-54; Bernadette Mbuy Beya, 'Human Sexuality, Marriage, and Prostitution', pp. 155-79, all in Onuyoye and Kanyoro (eds.), *The Will to Arise*.

over another. Failure to teach true equality between the two sexes, is failure to instill into society that the superiority of man over woman is contrary to God's intention for human beings. And today, indeed, there are some books and articles by African women theologians both in local and international publications that can be a resource giving fresh new gender perspectives to these old issues.

Accountability: An Issue for Churchwomen's Organizations

The best-known and longest serving Christian women's activism has been sustained through the Women's Desks of the Councils of Churches and the All Africa Council of Churches. The agenda carried out through such Desks have included strong elements of leadership training, social, economic and political analysis and gender conscientization. Whether it is women theologians or women who belong to pentecostal evangelical churches, most Christian women in Africa find it necessary to stay in the Church. The churches of Africa would be empty without women. It is right inside the Church that some choose to disturb the Church from within while looking for ways to nurture each other. This staying and talking from within is what gives meaning to mission and ministry from women's perspective. As in the rest of the world, some women are leaving churches because they are not able to put up with being in a church that does not make the needed changes quickly enough.[7] However, a majority of African women choose to stay active in church, even when the church is oppressive. While respecting the decisions of women who opt out of the Church, opting out of the Church for many of us is not a good choice because it gives the Church an excuse to deny women their God-given place in the Church. The clergy alone are not the Church. The leaders alone are not the Church. The Church is all the baptized people of God: children, women and men, ordained and laity, people with various physical and or economic disabilities. We are all the Church. How can this important 'body of Christ' be complete without women? It takes a lot of courage to keep our pain and struggles inside the Church, but it is worth the effort because in staying, we call the Church to accountability.

   In 1989, another very important continental churchwomen's organization held a remarkable assembly. Formed in 1987, the Pan African Christian

---

7.   Nokuzola Mdende, a Circle member from South Africa, has chosen to leave the Anglican Church together with some others and is trying to explore whether the traditional religion of her people offers more liberation for women. Her research will interest all of us, but she had to leave the Church because her search was seen as pagan.

Women's Assembly (PACWA) held its first assembly in 1989, in Nairobi, Kenya. The PACWA is the women's arm of the Association of Evangelicals of Africa and Madagascar, which is an association of evangelical churches. In terms of faith identity, a majority of Christian women in Africa would classify themselves as evangelicals in practice, even if they belong to historical churches. PACWA is therefore a very powerful organization which attracts women from churches throughout the continent. The theme of the PACWA assembly in 1989 was 'Our Time Has Come'.[8] In addition to spiritual and church issues, the assembly also had a very strong track of social issues such as family life, divorce, polygamy, social injustice, battering of women, child abuse, AIDS, sexual abuse, sorcery and an assortment of things which were grouped together as 'pagan practices'.

One could take issue on some of the stands of the PACWA on these issues, especially their blanket condemnation of things African as pagan, but overall, the mood of their conference was that of freeing African women from the bondage of culture. The Church should stay well connected to these prophetic signs if it wants to reach communities and those on the margins of communities. Further, PACWA planned to do post-assembly research on 'Economic and Cultural Issues Plaguing African Women'. These examples indicate that African women are seeking their own liberation. This is the hope for the women of Africa. *They are silenced but they are not silent*. Women in Africa value the message and call of Jesus Christ whom we have come to view as a liberator.[9]

Accountability: An Issue for African Women Theologians

In 1989, a group of women theologians met in Accra, Ghana, to create our movement of 'The Circle of Concerned African Women Theologians'. The theme of our convocation was 'Arise Daughter', taken from the act of Jesus raising a girl from death, found in Lk. 8.40-56. When Jesus raises one from death as he did the daughter of Jairus, it is such a shock treatment that it is difficult not to tell the story everywhere.[10] Sixty-nine women who were

---

8.   It also became the title of the book that was produced with the presentations to the assembly, Mbugua (ed.), *Our Time Has Come*.

9.   Teresa M. Hinga, 'Jesus Christ and the Liberation of Women in Africa', in Odoyoye and Kanoro (eds.), *The Will to Arise*), pp. 183-94.

10.   Teresa Okure 'Reflections on Luke 8.40-56', in Oduyoye and Kanyoro (eds.), *The Will To Arise*, pp. 221-30.

gathered in the Accra convocation arose and started writing and telling the stories of women in our communities. We jointly committed ourselves to correct the dearth of literature by African women on African religious and cultural issues. We vowed to narrow the chasm in the global knowledge about women in Africa. We decided that our Circle would be opened to any woman in Africa concerned about the well-being of and fullness of life for women in Africa. The research and writing of the Circle women has always to be seen in the context of human development that provides a network of communication among women while at the same time contributes to research that leads to positive policies and practices affecting women in Africa.

Our first continental volume, *The Will to Arise*, was published by Orbis in 1992. We have never gone back to slumber again. We are writing, speaking, preaching, studying the Bible and meeting to reject dehumanization of African women. Mercy Amba Oduyoye may be the most published African woman theologian, but she still serves as an oral consultant to many of us. She has been a torch to the continent, a woman who did not want to shine alone. The Circle for Concerned African Women Theologians came out of her vision. The vision was to initiate a forum which would enable African women to support each other to write. She shared this vision with many others, and today the Circle has a scattered membership all over the continent. Women write papers and then meet to present these papers to each other for joint critique. Some end up in books, while others appear in journals and yet others in the media. More than nine books have been produced since the launching in 1989.

The Circle has become for many of us a circle of solidarity. Talking about various research projects in the company of the Circle is important so that African women can help eradicate the dearth of literature from the continent. Professional death of trained scholars in Africa is the norm.[11] With a membership of about four hundred women from all over Africa extending from Cairo to Cape Town, the Circle members are doing theology in the context of their own setting. Currently, we are divided into four study commissions, namely:

1. Cultural and Biblical Hermeneutics
2. Women in Culture and Religion
3. History of Women
4. Ministry and Theological Education and Formation

---

11.   Musa W. Dube believes that professional death comes to third world people because they are trained in methods which stifle their own questions. This is discussed in her article, 'An Introduction: How We Come to Read with', *Semeia* 73, pp. 10-15.

Each commission has a team of two people who are trained in the discipline to coordinate the study. The coordination involves designing the nature of studies and inviting several members from different parts of Africa to carry out relevant field research on the topics identified and then write about it. For example, in her role as one of the study coordinators for Cultural and Biblical Hermeneutics, Musa Dube has begun to develop leadership in the area of post-colonial readings of the Bible. She comes to this subject with much experience gained from her graduate work in New Testament and in various liberation theologies.[12] She is but one of the new people that are bringing new life to the Circle theology.

Currently most of the writings of the Circle are in the form of articles and books. We have upgraded our newsletter, *AMKA*, to a journal and appointed editors for both an English and a French version. We have developed a directory of addresses and at the time of writing we are exploring possibilities for a web page. Many of the Circle members are connected to email and this is making communication between members, coordinators and other scholars easy and fast.

At the time of writing I am the general coordinator for all Circle events. I receive reports from the study commissions, update the address list and develop publicity materials. In this way, I have first-hand information of many aspects of the Circle work which prompts me to predict that within five years, African women will have enough material to show the significance of cultural hermeneutics.

The importance of the Circle theology is that we want to contribute something new to theology by bringing in the voices of women in Africa. Actions, such as the return to our villages of doing theology with our communities, make our work exciting. We do not stop at simply asking for some questions from our communities for research as has been done in the past. We stay with the issues, slowly discovering with the communities what the word of God is sending us to do. We examine that with feminist hermeneutical keys and then we engage ourselves practically in some form of change.

It is for this reason that women who belong to the Circle believe that the study of theology from the women's perspective is a gift to the Church and a gift to women. It is a gift to the Church because it calls the Church to repentance for its role in the subordination of women. It is a gift to women

12.   See, for example, Musa W. Dube, 'Reading for Decolonization (John 4.1-42)', *Semeia* 75 (1996), pp. 37-59; and also Gerald West and Musa W. Dube (eds.), 'Reading with: An Exploration of the Interface between Critical and Ordinary Reading of the Bible', *Semeia* 73 (1996).

because it has opened our eyes to the fact that the future of society and the future of women depend on our trusting the message of God rather than the message of men. We can read and interpret the Bible by ourselves and we can count on God's word that says God created men and women in God's own image (Gen. 1.27). The study of theology by women is the proverbial equivalent of the lion learning to write.   *ch. 6*

Theological reflections by women in Africa are still like an oasis in a desert because the number of theologians is still very small. They are therefore like a pearl of great value, a treasure long hidden and just discovered! Women have engendered theology by all its names—whether Systematic, Liberation, Inculturation, or Black Theology. Theology by women has valued and affirmed women's experiences in church and society. It gives women an imperative to call to memory their experiences by articulating their stories of faith and life in practical terms. Stories help to discover the interconnection between faith and action. The Bible, too, is about the stories of the Hebrew people and how they experienced and named their experience of God in their lives, in accordance with their faith in God.

Feminist and womanist theologies have helped women to discover that the God of the Bible is a God who liberates all people to worship and live together in community and in harmony. Living in harmony with one another implies that there is equal regard for one another and a mutual respect that does not leave room for considering one group of people inferior while another superior. The Bible was written in a patriarchal culture, very much like our African culture, where male values were exalted and female values despised. The fate that befell the women pioneers of the women's movements still follows the African women theologians using feminist methodology to work for change. Women in Africa have accepted and internalized subservient roles for centuries, and for anyone to question their validity is a disturbing phenomenon, easily condemned by both women and men alike. In Africa, to be associated with 'women's lib', raises aggression, resentment and mistrust in the African society at large and the Church specifically. It is especially dangerous in the family if a woman is seen to be interested in advocating for the rights of women. Husbands are embarrassed by wives who are activists. This alone can be a point of contention in a marriage relationship. The family in Africa is the nesting place for the gender subordination of women. The family is not only the nucleus of society, but also more importantly, the powerhouse of society.

Courageous women understand that to seek justice for women's well-being is a command from the Scriptures. Before God, all baptized people are worthy of the kingdom that Jesus' death announced. The Bible states that all have sinned. All have fallen short of glory. Christ died for all. This means *all* people, men and women alike, have received grace through Christ's death. To deny this grace to women is an injustice that requires a vigilant campaign to turn back to God's justice. For us women of Africa, the study of theology—any theology—first opens doors long closed on us. Theology creates a better understanding of the Scriptures that can affect the way women participate in group worship, as well as private personal meditation. When we look critically at our cultures, we know for certain that there are cases where our cultures dehumanize women. If we relate our study of culture to the Scriptures, we will find the power to speak to new lifestyles which reflect the justice of God for all people. In choosing culture as a departure point, we have the opportunity to start at home, in our hearts and in our various relations and settings.

To choose feminist theology as our method of study is to join a journey where we have solidarity with other women rather than keeping ourselves in a desert of risks and loneliness. We African women must see our struggles in the context of global gender injustice. This new experience gives us self-confidence—rootedness in oneself and in God. For African women, discovering and removing the obstacles on the way and creating new paths for the journey to freedom will come about through more contextualized holistic studies of the Scriptures with African women's eyes. We have been silent for much too long. To cry out and let the heavy burden we carry be shared through theologizing is our right! This is what makes this time a *kairos* moment for African women.

My connection to the community of Bware has only continued to grow. In 1994, I felt uncomfortable and even foreign to the people. Today, I no longer feel a foreigner. I feel at home because I have become part of the issues of Bware. The initial difficulties of my inabilities to cope with the strict apathy to culture is now replaced by faces and names and stories of women and their struggles which are handled with a dignity that a casual onlooker is likely to mistake for ignorance and apathy as I once did. But definitely the women of Bware will continue to need more reflection/action encounters. My task was to put in motion a process that can sustain itself. The groups that began in 1994 continue to exist in smaller units and they are studying the Bible and engaging in social action. I went back in 1996 as an invited guest and I continue to visit them when I am home or when I am invited.

This community has given me a space to use some of my resources both in kind and in cash. Through the group, I have realized that women may have constitutional rights, which are often overlooked or remain unknown. Improving the status of women is *the key* to development in Africa. It is paramount to improving health status, slowing the population growth and for economic and social progress. Investing in women leads to more rewarding lives for them, their families, communities and countries. Increasing the involvement of women at decision-making levels remains vital to long-term success in improving the status of women. This is dependent upon the availability of women with knowledge and skills required for these roles at these levels. Promoting the leadership of women is crucial. In my context, all of these things should be done in the context of how culture hinders women from making the needed progress to be the people that God made them to be. This is what doing theology means to me.

My interest in culture and feminist theology has led me to a renewed interest and appreciation of my own cultural roots. I find that as an African woman who is Christian, I can only understand myself through that triple heritage. However, I do not think that I can establish my identity through reading the biblical stories alone, nor can I do it through reclaiming the African religious faith alone. The reality invites me continuously to stage a dialogue between my two religious experiences and surely to make room around the table for other religious experiences with which I come in contact and to examine all of the above with a woman's lens.

The Bible provides the impetus and courage to go on even when the Church in Africa seems so far away from the mark. 'Then justice will dwell in the wilderness, and righteousness abide in the fruitful field. And the fruit of righteousness will be peace and the result of righteousness, undisturbed security for ever' (Isa. 32.15-17). The key words in this prophetic vision for a new world order are righteousness, justice, peace and undisturbed security. A just society depends on just people. A just society is one where men and women are equally united in their struggle and in their reward (loss or gain; success or failure); a society of true partnership among men and women, characterized by righteousness, justice, peace and undisturbed security. A just society is one in which men and women struggle equally and benefit equally. Gender roles are neither unchangeable nor divine. They must change over time as contexts change over time. This will not only enhance women's participation in social and political development, but it would also enhance and contribute to efficiency in utilization of resources and effectiveness of programs.

Biblical analysis by women has gone far to show that though women's stories seem few and far between in the biblical record, we can celebrate the rather miraculous fact that women like Deborah, Esther and Priscilla broke through limitations of patriarchy and helped shape history. Against all odds, they became a prophetess and judge over Israel, a queen who pleaded for and saved the lives of her people, and an articulate church leader who risked her life to save Paul's life. We have an African proverb, which says, 'If we stand tall, it is because we stand on the shoulders of those who were there before us.' Perhaps, with the knowledge that other women have gone courageously before us, we can refuse to be victims and claim our right to be God's dignified persons. A challenge to all others is, listen to the voices that are coming out of silence! To seek justice is to break the boundaries of injustice. The European theologian Dorothee Sölle says, 'The question posed by feminist liberation theology is not "Is there God?" but, "Does God happen among us, too?"'[13] Engendered cultural hermeneutics is about God happening among us, as African women who are daughters of God and daughters of Anowa.[14]

13.   Dorothee Sölle, 'Liberating Our God-Talk', in Ursula King (ed.), *Liberating Woman Conference Reader* (University of Bristol: European Society of Women for Theological Research, 1991).

14.   Mercy Amba Oduyoye, *Daughters of Anowa*. This book illustrates the struggle of Akan women in Ghana as they confront and affirm culture.

Bibliography

Achebe, Chinua, *Arrow of God* (London: Heinemann, 1964).

—*Things Fall Apart* (London: Heinemann, 1958).

Ackermann, Denis, *et al.* (eds.), *Women Hold Up Half the Sky: Women in the Church in Southern Africa* (Pietermaritzburg, 1991).

Adeyemo, Tokunboh, 'A Woman of Excellence', in Mbugua (ed.), *Our Time Has Come*, pp. 17-22.

Angogo-Kanyoro, R., *Unity in Diversity: A Linguistic Study of the ABALUHYIA of Western Kenya* (Vienna: Beiträge zur Afrikanistik, 20, 1983).

Ariarajah, S. Wesley, *Gospel and Culture: An Ongoing Discussion in the Ecumenical Movement* (Geneva: WCC Publications, 1994).

Atieno-P. Odhiambo, E.S., 'Some Aspects of Religiosity of the Boat Among the Luo of Uyoma', *Journal of East African Historical Association* (1973).

Baeta, C.G. (ed.), *Christianity and African Culture, Conference Report* (Accra, 1955).

Bailey, Randall C., and Tina Pippin, 'Race, Class, and the Politics of Biblical Translation', *Semeia* 76 (1996), pp. 1-6.

Bellis, Alice Ogden, *Helpmates, Harlots and Heroes: Women's Stories* (Louisville, KY: Westminster/John Knox Press, 1994).

Bird, Phyllis A., *The Bible as the Church's Book* (Philadelphia: Westminster Press, 1982).

Boulaga, F.E., *Christianity without Fetishes* (Maryknoll, NY: Orbis Books, 1984).

Brown, Cheryl Anne, *No Longer Be Silent* (Louisville, KY: Westminster/John Knox Press, 1990).

Brueggemann, Walter, *Interpretation and Obedience: From Faithful Reading to Faithful Living* (Minneapolis: Fortress Press, 1991).

Brunner, Leila Lear, *From Eve to Esther: Rabbinic Reconstruction of Biblical Women* (Louisville, KY: Westminster/John Knox Press, 1994).

Bruns, Gerald L., *Hermeneutics: Ancient and Modern* (New Haven: Yale University Press, 1992).

Bujo, Benezet, *African Theology in its Social Context* (Maryknoll, NY: Orbis Books, 1992).

Cannon, Katie G., *Black Womanist Ethics* (Atlanta: Scholars Press, 1988).

Cardenal, Ernesto, *The Gospel in Solentiname* (trans. Donald D. Walsh; 4 vols.; Maryknoll, NY: Orbis Books, 1982).

Carmody, Denise Lardner, *Biblical Woman* (New York: Crossroad, 1989).

Cohen, David William, and E.S. Atieno Odhiambo (eds.), *Siaya, The Historical Anthropology of an African Landscape: Eastern African Studies* (Nairobi: Heinemann, 1989).

Croato, Severino J., *Biblical Hermeneutics: Toward a Theory of Reading as the Production of Meaning* (trans. Robert R. Barr; Maryknoll, NY: Orbis Books, 1995).

Cunningham, Richard, 'Theologizing in a Global Context: Changing Contours', *Review and Expositor* 94.3 (1997), pp. 51-62.

Daly, Lois K., (ed.), *Feminist Theological Ethics: A Reader* (Louisville, KY: Westminster/John Knox Press, 1994).

Day, Peggy L. (ed.), *Gender and Difference in Ancient Israel* (Minneapolis: Fortress Press, 1993).

Donaldson, Laura E (guest ed. 'Postcolonialism and Scriptural Reading', *Semeia*, 1996).

Dube, Musa W., 'An Introduction: How We Come to Read With', *Semeia* 73 (1996), pp. 10-15.

Egbuji, Innocent I., 'The Hermeneutics of the African Traditional Culture' (PhD dissertation, Boston College, 1976).

Evans-Pritchard, E.E., *Theories of Primative Religion* (London: Oxford University Press, 1965).

Fabella, Virginia, and Mercy Oduyoye, *With Passion and Compassion: Third World Women Doing Theology* (Maryknoll, NY: Orbis Books, 1994).

Gibellini, Rosino (ed.), *Paths of African Theology* (London: SCM Press, 1994; Maryknoll, NY: Orbis Books, 1994).

Gnadadason, Aruna, Musimbi Kanyoro and Lucia Ann McSpadden, *Women, Violence and Non-Violent Change* (Geneva: WCC Publications, 1996).

Gottwald, Norman K., and Richard A. Horsley (eds.), *The Bible and Liberation: Political and Social Hermeneutics* (Maryknoll, NY: Orbis Books, 1993).

Hauge, H.E., *Luo Religion and Folklore* (Oslo: Sandinavian University Books, 1974).

—*Hermeneutics, Religious Pluralism and Truth* (Winston-Salem: Wake Forest Press, 1989).

Hick, John, and Paul F. Knitter (eds.), *The Myth of Christian Uniqueness: Towards a Pluralistic Theology of Religions* (Maryknoll, NY: Orbis Books, 1987).

Hinga, Teresa M., 'Jesus Christ and the Liberation of Women', in Odoyoye and Kanyoto (eds.), *The Will to Arise* (Tradition and the Church in Africa, Orbis Maryknoll, 1992), pp. 183-94.

Idowu, Bolaji, *African Traditional Religion: A Definition* (London: SCM Press, 1973).

Imasogie, O., *Guidelines for Christian Theology in Africa* (Accra: African Christian Press, 1983).

Isasi-Diaz, Ada Maria, *En La Lucha, In the Struggle: A Hispanic Women's Liberation Theology* (Minneapolis: Fortress Press, 1993).

Kanyoro, Musimbi R.A. (ed.), *In Search of a Round Table: Gender, Theology and Church Leadership* (Geneva: WCC Publications, 1997).

Kanyoro, Musimbi R.A., and Nyambura J. Njoroge (eds.), *Groaning in Faith: African Women in the Household of God* (Nairobi: Acton, 1996).

Kanyoro, Musimbi R.A., and Wendy Robins, *The Power We Celebrate: Women's Stories of Faith and Power* (Geneva: WCC Publications, 1992).

Kates, Judith A., and Gail Twersky Reimer (eds.), *Reading Ruth: Contemporary Women Reclaim a Sacred Story* (New York: Ballentine Books, 1994).

King, Noel, *Africa: African Cosmos—An Introduction to Religion* (Belmont: Wadsworth, 1986).

Kinoti, George, *Hope for Africa and What Christians Can Do* (Nairobi: AISRED Publications, 1994).

Kinoti, H.W., and J.M. Waliggo, *The Bible in African Christianity: Essays in Biblical Theology* (Nairobi: Acton, 1997).

Kirwen, Michael C., *African Widows* (Maryknoll, NY: Orbis Books, 1979).

Laffey, Alice L., *An Introduction to the Old Testament: A Feminist Perspective* (Philadelphia: Fortress Press, 1988).

Larom, Margaret S. (ed.), *Claiming the Promise: African Churches Speak* (New York: Friendship Press, 1994).

Laye, Camara, *The African Child* (London: Fontana, 1959).

Lorde, Audre, *Sister Outsider: Essays and Speeches* (Freedom: The Crossing Press, 1984).

Maimela, Simon S. (ed.), *Culture, Religion and Liberation* (All Africa Council of Churches African Challenges Series; Pretoria: Initiatives, 1994).

Malo, S., and G. William, *Luo and Customary Law* (Nairobi: Eagle Press, 1961).

Mananzan, Mary John, *et al.* (eds.), *Women Resisting Violence: Spirituality For Life* (Maryknoll, NY: Orbis Books, 1996).

Martey, Emmanuel, *African Theology: Inculturation and Liberation* (Maryknoll, NY: Orbis Books, 1993).

Mbiti, John S., *African Religions and Philosophy* (Nairobi: Heinemann, 1969).

Mboya, Paul, *Luo-Kitgi gi Timbega* (Kisumu: Anyanga Press, 1938).

Mbugua, Judy (ed.), *Our Time Has Come: African Christian Women Address the Issues of Today* (Grand Rapids: Baker Book House, 1994).

Mbula, Judith, 'Continuing Elements in African Traditional Religion in Modern Africa: The Case of Maweto Marriages in Ukambani' (Paper in manuscript form, Department of Philosophy and Religious Studies, University of Nairobi, 1975).

Mbuy Beya, Bernadette, 'Human Sexuality, Marriage, and Prostitution', in Oduyoye and Kanyoro (eds.), *The Will to Arise*, pp. 155-79.

Mojola, Aloo, *The Traditional Religious Universe of the Luo of Kenya: A Preliminary Study* (unpublished manuscript, 1994).

Mudflower Collective, *God's Fierce Whimsy: Christian Feminism and Theological Education* (New York: Pilgrim Press, 1985).

Mugambi, J., *African Heritage and Contemporary Christianity* (Nairobi: Longman, 1989).

Mugambi, J.N.K., and Laurenti Magesa (eds.), *The Church in African Christianity* (AACC Challenges Series; Nairobi: Initiatives, 1990).

Nida, Eugene A., *Religion Across Cultures* (New York: Harper & Row, 1968).

Nida, Eugene A., and William Reyburn, *Meaning Across Cultures* (Maryknoll, NY: Orbis Books, 1981).

Nida, Eugene A., and Charles D. Taber, *The Theory and Practice of Translation* (Leiden: E.J. Brill, 1969).

Njoroge, Nyambura J., 'Groaning and Languishing on Labour Pains: But for How Long Lord?', in Kanyoro and Njoroge (eds.), *Groaning in Faith*, pp. 3-15.

Ocholla-Ayayo, A.B.C. *Traditional Ideology and Ethics Among the Southern Luo* (Uppsala: Scandinavian Institute of African Studies, 1976).

Oduyoye, Mercy Amba, *Daughters of Anowa: African Women and Patriarchy* (Maryknoll, NY: Orbis Books, 1995).

—*Hearing and Knowing* (Maryknoll, NY: Orbis Books, 1986).

Oduyoye, Mercy Amba, and Musimbi R.A. Kanyoro (eds.), *The Will to Arise: Women, Tradition and the Church in Africa* (Maryknoll, NY: Orbis Books, 1992).

Ogot, B.A., *History of the Southern Luo* (London: Heinemann, 1967).

Oguda, L., *So They Say—The Luo Folklore* (Nairobi: East Africa Publishing House, 1967).

Okure, Teresa, 'Reflections on Luke 8.40-56', in Oduyoye and Kanyoro (eds.), *The Will to Arise*, pp. 221-30.

Ominde, S.H., *The Luo Girl from Infancy to Marriage* (London: Macmillan, 1967).

Ortega, Ofelia, *Women's Visions: Theological Reflection, Celebration, Action* (Geneva: WCC Publications, 1995).

P'Bitek, Okot, *Africa's Cultural Revolution* (Nairobi: Macmillan, 1973).

—*Religion of the Central Luo* (Nairobi: Macmillan, 1972).

Parrat, John, *Reinventing Christianity: African Theology Today* (Grand Rapids: Eerdmans, 1995).

Phiri, Isabel A., 'Women, Church, and Theological Education', *Ministerial Formation* 71 (Oct. 1995), pp. 39-43.

Plaskow, Judith, *Standing Again at Sinai: Judaism from a Feminist Perspective* (San Francisco: Harper & Row, 1991).

Pobee, John S., *Culture, Women and Theology* (Delhi: ISPEK, 1994).

—*Towards an African Theology* (Nashville: Abingdon Press, 1979).

Pobee, John S., and Barbel von Wartenberg-Potter, *New Eyes for Reading: Biblical and Theological Reflections by Women from the Third World* (Geneva: WCC Publications, 1986).

Ray, Benjamin, *African Religion—Symbol, Ritual, and Community* (Englewood Cliffs, NJ: Prentice–Hall, 1976).

Rebera, Ranjini, *Affirming Difference, Celebrating, Wholeness: A Partnership of Equals* (Hong Kong: Christian Conference of Asia, 1995).

—*The Book of Ruth: Creative Bible Study Guide* (New York: American Bible Society, 1998).

Reuther, Rosemary Radford, 'Feminism and Jewish–Christian Dialogue', in Hick and Knitter (eds.), *The Myth of Christian Uniqueness*.

Russell, Letty M., *Household of Freedom* (Philadelphia: Westminster Press, 1987).

—*The Church in the Round: Feminist Interpretation of Church* (Louisville, KY: Westminster/ John Knox Press, 1987).

Russell, Letty M. (ed.), *Feminist Interpretation of the Bible* (Philadelphia: Westminster Press, 1985).

Russell, Letty M., and J. Shannon Clarkson (eds.), *Dictionary of Feminist Theologies* (Louisville, KY: Westminster/John Knox Press, 1996).

Schüssler Fiorenza, Elisabeth, *Bread Not Stone: The Challenge of Feminist Biblical Interpretation* (Boston: Beacon Press, 1985).

—*But She Said: Feminist Practices of Biblical Interpretation* (Boston: Beacon Press, 1992).

Schüssler Fiorenza, Elisabeth (ed.), *The Discipleship of Equals: A Critical Feminist Ekklesiology of Liberation* (New York: Crossroad, 1993).

—*Searching the Scriptures: A Feminist Commentary* (2 vols.; New York: Crossroad, 1994).

Segovia, Fernando F., and Mary Ann Tolbert (eds.), *Reading from this Place: Social Location and Biblical Interpretation in Global Perspectives* (2 vols.; Minneapolis: Fortress Press, 1995).

—*Reading from this Place: Social Location and Biblical Interpretation in the United States* (Minneapolis: Fortress Press, 1995).

Sölle, Dorothee, 'Liberating Our God-Talk', in Ursula King (ed.), *Liberating Woman Conference Reader* (University of Bristol: European Society of Women for Theological Research, 1991).

Stic Services, *News Media and Information—Clip Service on Religion* (Stic Services, Box 402, Njoro, Kenya, 1987).

Tamez, Elsa, *Against Machismo* (Oak Park: Meyer/Stone, 1987).

—*The Amnesty of Grace: Justification by Faith from a Latin Perspective* (trans. Sharon H. Ringe; Nashville: Abingdon Press, 1993).

—*Bible of the Oppressed* (Maryknoll, NY: Orbis Books, 1979).

Tiffany, Frederick C., and Sharon H. Ringe, *Biblical Interpretation: A Road Map* (Nashville: Abingdon Press, 1996).

Virkler, Henry, *A Hermeneutic: Principles and Processes of Biblical Interpretation* (Grand Rapids: Baker Book House, 1981).

WCC Publication, *Living Letters: A Report of the Visits to the Churches During the Ecumenical Decade of Churches in Solidarity with Women* (Geneva: WCC Publications, 1997).

Weems, Renita, *Battered Love, Marriage, Sex and Violence in the Hebrew Prophets* (Minneapolis: Fortress Press, 1995).

—*Just A Sister Away: A Womanist Vision of Women's Relationships in the Bible* (San Diego, CA: Laura Media, 1988).

Welbourn, F.B., *A Place to Feel at Home* (Oxford: Oxford University Press, 1967).

Wendland, Ernst R., *The Culture Factor in Bible Translation: A Study of Communicating the Word of God in a Central African Context* (London: United Bible Societies, 1987).

West, Gerald, *Biblical Hermeneutics of Liberation: Modes of Reading the Bible in the South African Context* (Pietermaritzburg: Cluster Publication, rev. edn, 1995 [1991]).

West, Gerald, and Musa W. Dube (eds.), 'Reading with: An Exploration of the Interface between Critical and Ordinary Readings of the Bible', *Semeia* 73 (1996).

Williams, Delores S., *Sisters in the Wilderness: The Challenge of Womanist God-Talk* (Maryknoll, NY: Orbis Books, 1993).

Wiradu, Kwasi, *Philosophy and African Culture* (Cambridge: Cambridge University Press, 1980).

Zahan, Dominique, *The Religion, Spirituality and Thought of Traditional Africa* (trans. Kate Ezra and Lawrence M. Martin; Chicago: University of Chicago Press, 1979).

INDEXES

INDEX OF REFERENCES

OLD TESTAMENT

Genesis
1.27   91
2.23-24   86

Exodus
19–20   40
23.21-26   77

Leviticus
17–26   77
25   77
25.10   78

Deuteronomy
8.15-16   7
16–18   78
23.4-5   34

Ruth
1.16-17   32, 43
2.8   47
3.1-5   43
3.10-11   6
3.11   37

Isaiah
32.15-17   93

Matthew
5.3-12   77
15.21-28   7
28.18-20   72

Mark
7.31-38   7

Luke
4.18-19   37
6.20-25   77
6.20   56
7.1-10   7
8.40-56   88

John
4.1-42   90
8.3-11   8
10.10   37

1 Corinthians
9.19-23   73

INDEX OF AUTHORS

Achebe, C. 13, 25
Adeyemo, T. 36
Ariarajah, S.W. 12

Bahemuka, J.M. 86
Bellis, A.O. 35
Beya, B.M. 28, 86
Boraine, A. 79
Brunner, L.L. 34
Bujo, B. 9

Cannon, K.G. 27
Cardenal, E. 49
Croato, S.J. 9
Cunningham, R. 30

Daly, L.K. 71
Dube, M.W. 30, 89, 90

Evans-Pritchard, E.E. 14, 25

Fanusie, L. 86
Fiorenza, E.S. 76, 85
Freud, S. 63

Gibellini, R. 9, 14
Gottwald, N.K. 19

Hinga, T.M. 88
Horsley, R.A. 19

Isasi-Diaz, A.M. 27

Kanyoro, M.R.A. 14, 33, 86
Kates, J.A. 34
Kirwen, M.C. 36
Knoppers, A. 29

Laffey, A.L. 35
Laye, C. 25
Lorde, A. 72

Magesa, L. 10
Maimela, S.S. 9, 14, 25
Martey, E. 10
Mbiti, J.S. 62, 63
Mbugua, J. 88
Mbula, J. 60
Mojola, A. 51
Mudflower Collective 76
Mugambi, J.N.K. 10, 25
Nasimiyu-Wasike, A. 86
Njoroge, N.J. 30, 33, 84

Oduyoye, M.A. 14, 19, 26, 30, 64, 94
Okure, T. 88
Ortega, O. 27

P'Bitek, O. 56
Parrat, J. 10, 25
Phiri, I.A. 81
Plaskow, J. 34, 35
Pobee, J.S. 10, 14, 25

Rebera, R. 76
Reimer, G.T. 34
Ringe, S.H. 3, 19, 77
Robbins, W. 33
Ruether, R.R. 17, 64, 71, 73
Russell, L.M. 11, 77

Segovia, F.F. 19
Sölle, D. 94

Tiffany, F.C. 3, 19
Tolbert, M.A. 2, 19

Weems, R. 35
Wendland, E.R. 10
Williams, D.S. 27, 75

FEMINIST THEOLOGY TITLES

Individual Titles in Feminist Theology

Linda Hogan, *From Women's Experience to Feminist Theology*

Lisa Isherwood and Dorothea McEwan (eds.), *An A–Z of Feminist Theology*

Lisa Isherwood and Dorothea McEwan, *Introducing Feminist Theology*

Kathleen O'Grady, Ann L. Gilroy and Janette Patricia Gray (eds.), *Bodies, Lives, Voices: Gender in Theology*

Melissa Raphael, *Thealogy and Embodiment: The Post-Patriarchal Reconstruction of Female Sacrality*

Deborah Sawyer and Diane Collier (eds.), *Is There a Future for Feminist Theology?*

Lisa Isherwood (ed.), *The Good News of the Body: Sexual Theology and Feminism*

Alf Hiltebeitel and Kathleen M. Erndl, *Is the Goddess a Feminist? The Politics of South Asian Goddesses*

Introductions in Feminist Theology

Rosemary Ruether, *Introducing Redemption in Christian Feminism*

Lisa Isherwood and Elizabeth Stuart, *Introducing Body Theology*

Melissa Raphael, *Introducing Thealogy: Discourse on the Goddess*

Pui-lan Kwok, *Introducing Asian Feminist Theology*

Janet H. Wootton, *Introducing a Practical Feminist Theology of Worship*

Mary Grey, *Introducing Feminist Images of God*

Mercy Amba Oduyoye, *Introducing African Women's Theology*

Lisa Isherwood, *Introducing Feminist Christologies*

Feminist Companion to the Bible (1st Series)

Athalya Brenner (ed.), *A Feminist Companion to the Song of Songs*

Athalya Brenner (ed.), *A Feminist Companion to Genesis*

Athalya Brenner (ed.), *A Feminist Companion to Ruth*

Athalya Brenner (ed.), *A Feminist Companion to Judges*

Athalya Brenner (ed.), *A Feminist Companion to Samuel–Kings*

Athalya Brenner (ed.), *A Feminist Companion to Exodus–Deuteronomy*

Athalya Brenner (ed.), *A Feminist Companion to Esther, Judith and Susanna*

Athalya Brenner (ed.), *A Feminist Companion to the Latter Prophets*

Athalya Brenner (ed.), *A Feminist Companion to the Wisdom Literature*

Athalya Brenner (ed.), *A Feminist Companion to the Hebrew Bible in the New Testament*

Athalya Brenner and Carole Fontaine (eds.), *A Feminist Companion to Reading the Bible: Approaches, Methods and Strategies*

Feminist Companion to the Bible (2nd Series)

Athalya Brenner and Carole Fontaine (eds.), *Wisdom and Psalms*

Athalya Brenner (ed.), *Genesis*

Athalya Brenner (ed.), *Judges*

Athalya Brenner (ed.), *Ruth and Esther*

Athalya Brenner (ed.), *Samuel and Kings*

Athalya Brenner (ed.), *Exodus–Deuteronomy*

Athalya Brenner (ed.), *Prophets and Daniel*